Changing
the
Curriculum

lewis b. mayhew

patrick j. ford

foreword by winfred l. godwin

changing the
curriculum

Jossey-Bass Publishers
San Francisco · Washington · London · 1973

CHANGING THE CURRICULUM
by Lewis B. Mayhew and Patrick J. Ford

Copyright © 1971 by Jossey-Bass, Inc., Publishers

Published and copyrighted in Great Britain by
Jossey-Bass Publishers
3 Henrietta Street
London WC2E 8LU

Library of Congress Catalogue Card Number LC 79-159265

International Standard Book Number ISBN 0-87589-104-7

Manufactured in the United States of America

JACKET DESIGN BY WILLI BAUM

FIRST EDITION:
     First printing: September 1971
     Second printing: January 1973

Code 7124

The
Jossey-Bass Series
in Higher Education

Consulting Editors

JOSEPH AXELROD
*San Francisco State College
and University of California, Berkeley*

MERVIN B. FREEDMAN
*San Francisco State College
and Wright Institute, Berkeley*

Foreword

The story is told of a distinguished educator who some years ago accepted the academic deanship of a bustling state college in a southern state. The president of the college said to him, "You will have a free hand in this job—make whatever changes you see fit to make. Just don't monkey around with the curriculum!" The story tells a great deal about higher education in the last two decades, for this president's attitude typifies the faith in the basic soundness of the American higher educational structure and process which animated educators during the 1950s.

The volatile educational decade of the 1960s may have shattered for many this faith in conventional practices of colleges and universities. Many who did sense that something had somehow gone wrong with the higher educational enterprise were inclined to blame enrollment growth or changes in educational clientele or the new attitudes associated with the so-called youth counterculture or the mismanagement of college administrators—and not to question curriculum structure and content. Others were painfully aware of the rigidities characterizing much of the higher educational operation in spite of the rapidly accelerating changes of society at large.

Lewis Mayhew began to think and write about the nature

of the curriculum and of related educational matters at least as far
back as the early 1950s. The inflexible curriculum appeared to him
a major obstacle to educational progress long before campus unrest sparked new interest in the relevance of academic programs.
Mayhew's association with the Southern Regional Education Board
(SREB) spans more than a decade, beginning with membership
on an advisory committee for the study of the humanities in the
colleges and universities in the South. His specific interest in the
college curriculum involved him in several SREB meetings and the
subsequent publication under SREB auspices of four research monographs. Three are now out of print, but happily *Changing the
Curriculum* develops a unitary treatment of the overall topic of
curriculum reorganization and integrates the essential propositions
of those studies.

        This contribution of Mayhew and Patrick Ford does not
presume to present a simple set of answers to a difficult problem.
It does offer guidelines to the search in which educators must always
remain in order to keep abreast of the social and individual needs
the college curriculum must serve if it is to be effective.

Atlanta   WINFRED L. GODWIN
September 1971   *President*
                                   Southern Regional Education Board

Preface

In *Changing the Curriculum* we try to bring together the results of a decade or more of study of undergraduate curricula. During the 1960s more research about college students, the impact of college, and the results of curriculum experimentation was produced than in any other period of time, and probably more than has been produced in the entire history of higher education. We have tried to be aware of this research and to point out implications of principal findings for curriculum development and for teaching. Throughout our book we have tried to keep in mind faculty members and administrators who struggle with issues of curriculum revision and reform. While there are some idealistic portions in the book, we have sought to maintain an applied focus, suggesting, for example, how theories from developmental psychology can be applied in a college situation.

The thesis of our book is that the college curriculum can be considerably more than an aggregate of courses offered as professorial interests dictate. The curriculum should be based upon

human needs and structured to make educational sense to students
and managerial sense to those responsible for administration. The
attitudes toward the curriculum are reforming but not radical.

Stanford, California   LEWIS B. MAYHEW
September 1971   PATRICK J. FORD

Contents

Changing
the
Curriculum

Issues,
Practices, and
New Models

Perhaps never before has American higher education been in the flux it is today as the enterprise reacts to the pressures and problems of larger numbers of students, higher costs, increased knowledge, and greater demand for services. As colleges and universities struggle to adapt techniques and programs to new conditions, the curriculum becomes a major focus of attention. This discussion attempts to criticize the major existing ways of thinking about the curriculum and to suggest some principles by which curriculum problems might be solved.

The solution to the curriculum problems of an institution might take into consideration a number of transcendent issues that are as old as the arguments against the Sophists by Socrates and as new as the difference between Clark Kerr's conception of the multiversity and Robert M. Hutchins' continued emphasis on the liberal arts. Whether these issues can be resolved definitively is moot, but they must be accommodated in any curriculum scheme.

First among these issues is culture versus utility. Should the college stress, as the colonial college did, classical literature, moral philosophy, and natural philosophy, which were designed to shape the mind and form the character, or should it stress the application of knowledge to specific tasks, whether agricultural, engineering, or legal? Should a modern liberal arts college use its resources to offer a nonvocational experience in the liberal arts and sciences, or should it concentrate on preparing students to do something, whether it be to teach, enter business, or succeed in graduate school?

Then there is the general versus the specific. Should students be introduced to broad views of domains of knowledge, or should they be required to concentrate their efforts in a limited field? The issue seems involved in Jerome Bruner's emphasis on the structure of knowledge as contrasted with the behavioristic concentration on specific patterns which B. F. Skinner prefers. It is also involved in the struggle between the emphasis of the departments on single-discipline courses and the pleas of theorists for broad interdisciplinary work. It is clearly reflected when one contrasts the theory that underlies general education courses in natural science with the belief of Joel Hildebrand that generalization should and can come only after a student has been immersed in details.

A third issue derives from the second. Should the curriculum be open or closed, elective or prescribed? If one takes the stance that there are common elements of culture which all must share and which it is the duty of the college to convey, one moves toward a prescribed curriculum. The Sophists did that with their concentration on dialectic, rhetoric, and grammar; in 1828 the Yale faculty did it with the statement "that our prescribed course contains only those subjects which ought to be understood, as we think, by every-one who aims at a thorough education." The University of Chicago, Michigan State University, and St. John's College did the same thing with their required cores of general education. But one can take the opposite view and hold with Charles W. Eliot that each student should be allowed to study what interests him and that each professor should be free to teach what he wants to teach.

The fourth issue is whether college education should be designed for the elite or for everyone. In terms of broad policy this issue may no longer seem relevant in a time when statements such as that of the Educational Policies Commission call for universal higher education at least through the fourteenth grade. But for specific curriculum decisions it seems as relevant now as it did in 1828, when the Yale faculty argued that a college education was not for everyone. Russell Kirk argues the same line with his suggestion that "the colleges should return to a concise curriculum emphasizing classical literature, languages, moral philosophy, history, the pure sciences, logic, rhetoric, and religious knowledge."[1] Kirk clearly acknowledges that such a curriculum is not for everyone, but rather for those destined for leadership. For lesser people he would reluctantly tolerate state-supported schools or no formal schooling beyond high school. The public junior college wavers in its curriculum choices because of the same issue. Should it emphasize a transfer curriculum with elitist connotations or a terminal and technical program, which is more egalitarian in essence?

Then there is the problem of whether courses and programs should be oriented to the student or to the subject. A student-oriented curriculum exists principally to bring about changes in human personality. It regards the processes of education as of greater worth than the substance—indeed, there can be many substances. Such things as prerequisites and sequences are of much less importance than is the validity of a course in the light of what students want and need. Although few professors would claim that the subject is valid even without students, many nevertheless give the impression that this is true. They feel with Mark Van Doren that "it is [the professor's] subject; he spends his life thinking about it, whether in or out of class; it is his second if not his first nature; it is what gives him joy. No student ever fails to be aware of this. The truly personal teacher is the most responsible to his subject. Because he knows it to be more important than himself, he is humble in its presence and

[1] R. Kirk, *The Intemperate Professor* (Baton Rouge, La.: State University Press, 1966), p. 56.

would rather die than misrepresent it. It existed before him and will exist after him; its life is long, though his is short."[2]

A related question is whether the curriculum, or significant parts of it, should be discipline-centered or problem-centered. Does one teach the young a set of skills and approaches which they will later employ to solve problems, or should they be encouraged to look at problems and develop skills as needed? Should courses in statistics or historiography precede consideration of research problems, or should the techniques needed derive from the raising of questions? If one favors a discipline orientation, the curriculum can be developed logically and sequentially from courses dealing with terminology to those at higher levels. Only at the apex does one look at concrete problems. But if one takes the opposite stance, a freshman course on the problems of teenage drug use or one on conflict resolution would be supported.

In the United States this issue takes the form of whether to emphasize only the Western tradition or to include significant non-Western elements. In theory, the issue seems to have been resolved in favor of the cosmopolitan view, though this is not fully implemented. The most frequently taught courses in history are American and Western European civilization; in political science, they are American government and international affairs (which translated is Western European power politics). The continued existence of the issue even at the theoretical level is shown by Gordon Chalmers' remark that the values of the non-West are recognized when they support the basic values of the West.

The last issue is whether the sciences or the humanities should characterize the undergraduate curriculum. Theorists argue that students should have experience in both. Again, in theory, at least for the moment, the issue seems resolved, but read *scientism* for *science* and the matter comes to life again. Should courses be taught as laboratory exercises in which the disciplines of science are stressed, or should they be of a philosophic nature? Should courses in history, sociology, or psychology be taught as approaches to under-

[2] M. Van Doren, "The Good Teacher," in H. A. Estrin and D. M. Goode (Eds.), *College and University Teaching* (Dubuque, Iowa: Brown, 1964), p. 40.

standing or as scientific methods of dealing with small segments of reality? Graduate education seems to be in the science camp, as suggested by William Arrowsmith's diatribe about graduate work in the humanities. And the fact that colleges seem reluctant to embrace in a significant way the practice of art implies a leaning toward science. This tendency was not always present. Special colleges had to be created to allow science into the early nineteenth century curriculum, and Eliot's free election system was in a sense a stratagem to give the sciences an opportunity to compete.

If one examines recent attempts at curriculum construction, one finds a struggle to accommodate all these issues. The general education movement (reflected in the sixteen-course plan at the College of the University of Chicago, the program at the University College of Michigan State, and the efforts of Harvard College described in *General Education in a Free Society*) was a movement away from free election, subject-centeredness, specific training, discipline orientation, utilitarianism, and elitism. Out of that movement grew interdisciplinary courses which focused on problems of significance to students. Some defined general education as roughly similar to the concept of the liberal arts and sciences but without the aristocratic connotations of the term. And the general education stress upon the nonvocational parts of man's life revealed that vocationalism either had gone too far or perhaps was no longer needed.

During the 1930s and 1940s experimental colleges enjoyed a healthy development, and those schools revealed another resolution of fundamental issues. Such colleges as Bennington, Bard, Sarah Lawrence, Antioch, Stephens, and Reed emphasized curricula based on student needs. During the first few years at Bennington, for example, no courses were even listed in the catalog. At Sarah Lawrence, students were expected to select, with the help of advisers, broad areas of inquiry into which they delved in ways that made sense to them. These schools also made serious efforts to establish the performing arts; ballet, painting, dramatic creation, and creative writing were developed and encouraged in spite of the general belief that those courses were not academically appropriate for colleges. Much of the success of these experimental programs was expected to come not from the courses themselves but from the intimate interaction with a tutor, don, or adviser. Education was seen as a process not unlike the process of psychotherapy, which does not reveal truth but rather brings about a changed set of relationships. The similarity is no accident. The idea implicit in these experimental colleges represents a confluence of John Dewey's pragmatism and Freudian psychology.

A different order of curriculum movement was the cooperative education program. In 1906 the University of Cincinnati began a program in which students combined work and study in an integrated fashion. Gradually the movement expanded and finally received legislative recognition with funds made available by the Higher Education Act of 1965. As colleges embraced cooperative work-study as a curriculum ideal, they saw a number of values: by relating theory and practice, education was tied closely to student needs; jobs added motivation to student study; the work experience developed desirable character traits; mingling with workers developed a democratic understanding of others; the work experience pointed toward a life of work and motivated students for it; because the work was paid employment, it encouraged the education of students who otherwise could not afford to attend college; contacts with business and industry helped professors make their courses practical.[3]

The curriculum developments in liberal arts colleges have been of quite a different order. In two studies certain liberal arts colleges were found to be unusually productive of people who subsequently entered graduate schools. This finding, coupled with an unprecedented post-World War II demand for college education, enabled a number of these schools virtually to become graduate preparatory schools. Such low-level vocational curricula as home economics, business, and elementary education were deemphasized, and in their places were put sequences of courses which would prepare young people for success in graduate schools. Programs in the sciences and mathematics were strengthened, and courses in the humanities were made more analytical and scientific than they had pre-

[3] J. W. Wilson and E. H. Lyons, *Work-Study College Programs* (New York: Harper and Row, 1961), pp. 1–2.

viously been. The large pool of applicants made selectivity possible, and so these colleges, using the services of the College Entrance Examination Board, sought only students who could survive a highly academic program. This practice usually conflicted with the desires of the departments stressing the performing arts, because students with acting or musical talent frequently do not possess the interest or abilities to succeed in courses designed as preludes to graduate and professional study. Those in the arts generally lost.

Because research in graduate schools was producing an expansion of the number of fields and specialties, the liberal arts curriculum was expanded to keep pace. Typically, interdisciplinary courses of a general education nature were sacrificed because faculties preferred to teach specialized courses, claiming that this was what the graduate or professional school wanted. So widespread has been the adoption of this curriculum, even in schools which do not send many graduates to graduate schools, that Earl McGrath suggests there has been a decline of liberal education. Further, he points to the elite side of the development: "Selective admission on limited measures of ability to pass achievement tests may close the door of opportunity to those who have the capacity to innovate, to conceive imaginative approaches to the solution of problems, to recognize, interrelate, and resystematize the findings of several branches of knowledge, or who have a dedication to human welfare that will result in singular contributions to the well being of mankind."[4]

A peculiar curriculum effort, in the light of the issues, is the honors program. An early manifestation was the creation of the pass-honors degree at Swarthmore in 1922, but the program did not gain headway until the American public, prompted by Russian scientific achievements climaxed by Sputnik in 1957, demanded rigor in education. Generally honors programs are intended for the intellectually gifted, hence in one sense they are elitist. But many of the honors courses are broad, stress important questions, raise value issues, accept the conflicts which college students experience, and try to focus their attention on ends. Honors courses seek to

[4] E. J. McGrath, *The Liberal Arts College and the Emergent Caste System* (New York: Teachers College Press, 1966), p. 22.

place work in a broad context and to help students to establish relationships between their lives and what they study.

Then there are the house plan or cluster college experiments. These typically seek to bring a limited number of students and faculty together to follow either a prescribed curriculum or a common curriculum based on the desires of the group. Generally the students live in a residence hall which also contains classrooms, faculty offices, and sometimes even a small library collection. The concept is based on the idea that strong primary group relationships among students and faculty can make the intellectual content of the curriculum more meaningful than it generally is; hence the concept is student-centered. The courses, even when prescribed, are usually attempts at interdisciplinary synthesis. With few exceptions, however, the curricula are Western European or American in orientation. (A mild exception is the Covell campus of the University of the Pacific, which is Pan American in outlook, offering courses in Latin and North American cultures usually taught in Spanish and English to students recruited from both cultures.)

The most frequently cited examples of cluster colleges and house plans are those lodged in teaching-oriented institutions. Stephens College, the College of Basic Studies of Boston University, the Raymond Campus of the University of the Pacific, and the New College of Hofstra University are all well described and seem generally to have worked. Similar attempts are now being made in the context of research-oriented universities. Stanford is creating its Stern House, and Joseph Tussman is conducting an experimental college at the University of California, Berkeley. At Harvard, seminars are a modified attempt to achieve similar ends. Since the faculties at such institutions are oriented toward their disciplines, relying on department status to gain the rewards of promotion and recognition, there is some question as to whether the efforts can be sustained. Here is a stark illustration of the dilemma presented by several of the issues—a subject-centered faculty attempting to offer a student-centered curriculum.

Another curriculum form which has been frequently attempted is an integrating course or seminar to help students bring together the various strands of their college experience. An early example of this attempt was the senior course at the University of Chicago, which was generally well regarded and received. It had the advantages of following a prescribed core of integrated general education courses. To offer such a course at the end of a curriculum which featured specialized single-discipline courses has proven difficult. The integrating course demands an instructor who has a broad awareness of interrelationships among various subjects, which few professors seem to possess. Then, it must speak to students in non-vocational terms at the time in their lives when they must begin to anticipate life outside college, when they are becoming anxious about their vocations.

A number of colleges have attempted to resolve curriculum issues through manipulation of the academic calendar. While institutions such as the University of Pittsburgh and the state-supported institutions of Florida adopted the trimester for economic reasons, other institutions have used modifications to compensate for imbalances in their programs. Earlham adopted the three-three plan, which allows students to spend concentrated periods on a limited number of subjects but still provides flexibility so that students can pursue individual interests. Another pattern is the four-one-four plan, which provides intensive on-campus study for four months, then a month for individual work off campus, followed by four more months of formal on-campus experience. A variant of this pattern, used by Mount Holyoke, is one which provides for two long terms followed by one shorter term. Students work on their majors and other requirements during the two long terms and use the short last term to take one course each year of an exploratory or synthesizing nature.

There are, of course, many more experiments. Wellesley has cut the number of courses a student may take from five to four and has made one of the four in each of the freshman and sophomore years a large lecture course with no discussion section. This scheme is economically sound and it is intended to train students to learn in large groups and to assume full responsibility for out-of-class preparation. Stanford offers elective senior courses, taught by major professors, which attempt to expose broad issues. These courses and titles change from year to year as student demands and interests change. A number of colleges have developed overseas experiences to provide small-group compensation for the impersonal life on campus and to break excessive parochialism.

In addition to these established curriculum efforts to resolve fundamental education issues, there are a number of what might be called emergent attempts. The free university idea is one. Students, finding that college courses organized by discipline did not respond to the significant questions their own needs posed, have begun to band together outside the structure of the university and to create courses of a broad interdisciplinary nature. Gathering in and around large cities like New York and San Francisco, these clusters of students and some faculty have attempted to explore the bases of the war in Viet Nam and the problems of a segregated society, censorship, and similar problems. The ideological rationale for these efforts is presented by Paul Goodman, who utopianly believes that administrative structure can be avoided and that all students who seriously want an education can obtain one through such groups.

The definite political bias, usually to the left, of some curriculum content is clear, but it would be wrong to assume that the free university concept is invalid. The select faculty committee of the University of California at Berkeley finds that a number of brilliant students reject the formalism of the university, become nonstudents, and then engage in more serious intellectual effort than before. To meet the needs of that group, the committee recommended that "the administration should arrange for ad hoc courses, the topics of which may be determined from term to term by the Board of Educational Development, to supply the relevant scholarly and intellectual background to subjects of active student concerns."[5] Courses on the city and Sino-Soviet-American relations illustrate the expected demand.

There is a developing interest in the performing arts as essential elements of academic life, not just for the professional but for all members of the academic community. Until recently students were generally exposed to art, music, or drama appreciation which focused on the historical evolution of art forms. But the contempo-

[5] University of California, Berkeley Academic Senate, *Education at Berkeley, Report of the Select Committee on Education* (Berkeley, Calif.: University of California, 1966), p. 128.

rary interest in op and pop art, in happenings, in homemade textiles, and in folk dancing reveals a creative urge to which the curriculum should speak. Colleges and universities are responding by sponsoring festivals of the arts such as at Stanford, Michigan State, and Olivet, and by assuming leadership in the preparation of professionals in all the arts. Even in fields such as drama and motion pictures the university is taking the place of technical or specialized schools of art. For example, fewer professional dramatic schools flourish in the 1970s than did several decades earlier, although the number of students has increased significantly. Gradually universities are also beginning to support and present the work of mature artists both to subsidize the artists and to expose the entire community to opera, music, dance, theater, and painting.

Even more gradually colleges and universities are beginning to encourage through the curriculum active student participation in the arts, even when students have no professional pretensions. At the University of South Florida each student who takes the course in humanities is required to take a studio course, preferably in an art form with which he is unfamiliar. When planners developed St. Andrews College they urged that each student work on some project, again preferably of an aesthetic or creative nature. The time may come when curriculum emphasis on the creative and the imaginative might even exceed the current emphasis on the critical and the analytical, especially if, as some have suggested, survival in the future depends on the ability to use leisure rather than the ability to earn a living. Although it may be repugnant to the classical academician, college credit is being assigned for weaving, basket making, and dabbling with paint.

Another emergent development is the attempt to restructure freshman and sophomore courses in the sciences, social sciences, and mathematics to conform to new research concepts and to fundamental changes in secondary school curricula. These efforts move away from taxonomic or descriptive treatment of separate subjects toward combinations which seek to establish base structures for fields. One clear implication of this development is that smaller undergraduate colleges can probably offer a more balanced and respectable program with fewer courses than they could when the emphasis was on the discretely descriptive. An example might be the combination into a single course of the first year of chemistry and physics or of botany and zoology.

The reestablishment of religion and theology as important parts of the curriculum is another development, the dimensions of which are only dimly seen at the present. Secular institutions are creating departments of religion and theology which, when properly staffed, attract heavy enrollment in their elective courses. In church-related schools required work in theology is being updated in its idiom and relevance. Roman Catholic schools, for example, are finally paying attention to student criticism of work in dogmatic theology. Well prepared theologians are being assigned to teach, and the belief that any priest can teach theology has, for the most part, been rejected. Further, the new theology seeks to be congruent with the student's psychology and his existential situation—theology is being brought into harmony with the realities of the last third of the twentieth century. The reason behind this effort is that students are searching for meaning which older structures do not provide. The ready response to serious efforts to establish meaning and relevance through religion and philosophy suggests that, even in a secular age which four or five years ago proclaimed the "death of God" doctrine, still has much influence and some form of theology is needed.

There is a growing interest in independent study as a way of stretching inadequate faculty resources and letting the curriculum become relevant to the specific interests and talents of individual students. (We do not mean the tutorial system within which students meet the instructor each week. That is a different matter and speaks to different needs.) Independent study plans are attempts to allow the student to decide what is important to him, to formulate a plan for its elaboration, and to work until he is personally satisfied with the outcome. In its more orthodox form this independent study consists of working on some scholarly or research project, sometimes during an intersession period. But the emerging form allows wide latitude for students to acquire academic credit for such activities as a summer in civil rights work or a mountain climbing field trip for which the student also receives pay. The new plans are based on a growing acceptance of the point that many experiences outside the classroom have educational value. Teaching grade school children in a depressed area, a summer of concentrated reading, registering voters in the South, or free-lance writing can all have curriculum significance.

It should be clear, just from this enumeration of curriculum efforts, that no resolution of basic issues has yet been accomplished. Further, resolution is not likely, for the issues are rooted in man's condition, in the flux of life, and in society. However, each institution and each professor must attempt to resolve the issues. To assist in this process, several suggestions are made.

First, institutions should recognize that the undergraduate college is neither a graduate nor a professional school. Nevitt Sanford points out that the period of late adolescence is a distinct stage in which people have discrete needs. Too frequently the undergraduate curriculum does not recognize such a premise and courses are either relevant to secondary schools or appropriate for specialized graduate or technical work. Sanford argues that college freshmen need the opportunity to expand "impulsivity," yet they are forced to concentrate on single-discipline courses. Instead of rhetoric, inorganic chemistry, algebra, and history, freshmen should take courses in literature, philosophy, and the arts. Whether Sanford's specific formulation is correct, the point can still be stressed that if the undergraduate college persists in applying graduate school solutions to undergraduate problems, Jacques Barzun's prediction of the end of undergraduate liberal arts colleges may well come true.

The second suggestion is that the needs of undergraduates can be identified by watching what they do outside the formal curriculum. Out of the extracurriculum have come such essentials to the college scene as libraries, fraternities, intercollegiate athletics, dramatics, music, and speech. In the future it may be possible to shape the curriculum nearer to the needs of students if one can infer from student psychology and from student out-of-class behavior what they want and need. This is no easy prescription, for students say and do many contradictory things, but the faculty can listen with the "third ear" of the therapist and possibly infer correctly.

The majority of students will not provide the answers. They are, as they have been for several decades, self-centered, passive, resistant to change, and willing to tolerate classes and study in exchange for the symbols of a college degree. The student minority, however, is saying many things. These students are critical of the American value system, which tolerates affluence and a caste system; they resent teachers who would be happier if students did not exist; they expect a revealing college experience, only to discover that many courses are dry reruns of secondary school courses. From these bright, well-prepared but disillusioned students possible answers to curriculum questions may be found. Even the demands for sexual freedom, the experiments with drugs, and the teach-ins probably have meaning for the curriculum if they can be interpreted correctly.

To make wise interpretations of how well the existing curriculum is working and what student expectations are, use should be made of several sets of eyes. Faculties and administrations looking at the curriculum in their corporate capacities very often see a limited side of the matter. (This is the only charitable way to explain the heated debate in faculty meetings about such issues as a one-year language requirement, the need for classes to meet the prescribed number of hours, a no-cut policy, the justifications for specialized advanced courses, and whether a major should consist of twenty-five or thirty hours of credit.) If an anthropologist in his professional capacity were to review the curriculum, he might find that it is not language facility that is desired from a particular requirement but the suffering from a rite of passage. An ecologist looking at how the total campus functions might discover relationships between groups, buildings, and the surrounding community which are furthered by seemingly nonrational curriculum requirements. And even a cartoonist looking at the curriculum certainly could spot and illustrate inanities. This need for different sets of eyes to view the curriculum is responsible for the current popularity of consultants.

It may be that the computer, making application of systems or game theory, could have considerable relevance for curriculum decisions and curriculum structure. System analysis might be described as a method for determining "(1) where, when, with what, and with whom (2) you must accomplish (3) what, for whom, and where."[6] The purpose of this kind of analysis "is to provide

[6] D. G. Ryan, "System Analysis in Planning," in O. A. Knorr (Ed.),

cues and suggestions leading to a system or design or to system modification or redesign."[7] While no college or university has yet sought to apply systems theory to itself or its curriculum, the capability for dealing with complex problems suggests an ultimate use.

In reaching curriculum decisions, an institution should consider a variety of evidence: (1) students' characteristics, traits, desires, and needs; (2) graduates' performance, characteristics, attitudes, and reflections about their college experience; (3) faculty members' ages, abilities, interests, development, and motivations; (4) the cost of courses, departments, divisions, colleges, recruitment, equipment, and overall operation; (5) the expectations of those who use a product of the college—employers, husbands and wives, the military; (6) the expectations of the larger society; (7) the changing character of society and, more important, the rate and direction of change; (8) practices elsewhere and assessment of experienced gains and losses; (9) patterns of progress through the college years.

Long Range Planning in Higher Education (Boulder: Western Interstate Commission for Higher Education, 1965), p. 109, citing R. M. Davis, "Techniques of System Design," in E. M. Bennet (Ed.) *Military Information Systems* (New York: Praeger, 1965).

[7] Ryan, p. 107.

II

Student
Search for
Self

In addition to the suggestions offered in the previous chapter, curriculum builders should be aware of the developmental needs of contemporary college students.

College students seek to learn to make decisions for themselves about such crucial problems as marriage, a major, and a vocation. However, they testify that they receive little help from parents, secondary school, or college. Many students simply drift into a major and, although they testify that they are reasonably sure they have selected wisely, the fact that they shift majors so frequently is proof that they have not. Illustrative of this indecision is the statement of one student:[1]

I decided on chemical engineering as a major during my senior year in high school. As a matter of fact, I decided when I was filling out my application that fall. We were asked to put down what we intended to major in. Since I had such an interest in science and math, I felt my major should be somewhere in that category, and I liked chemistry so well—I thought that would be a good way to start. After I got into algebra in ninth grade, I had always thought that my future plans should have something to do with math, because I've always liked math, and always did quite well in math. But I hadn't really considered chemical engineering until my senior year. In my junior year, the only thing I was sure of was that [my major] was going to be something in science and math. I don't have any idea as to why chemical engineering, rather than chemistry, physics, or some other science. As a matter of fact, when I put down chemical engineering I hardly knew what it was, except that it dealt with chemistry. I still think that's kind of my general idea of it. I can go ahead and take courses for at least two years, and then either become a chemist or a chemical engineer. I think I probably put down chemical engineering mainly because I enjoyed physics, and a chemical engineer employs more math and more physics than a pure chemist.

This same indecision is reflected by another:[2]

Well, I think the biggest obstacle, or whatever you want to call it, is that I'm not sure exactly what I want to do. There's no problem right now, because I don't have any decision to make right now. But the problem would be whether I would go on to get a graduate degree . . . and then go on into a profession, or whether I'd be willing to settle down. This question may never come up, but I think that even if it did come up, it would be a hard decision to make, because I've always wanted to have an outside career.

[1] P. Madison, "Dynamics of Development and Constraint: Two Case Studies," in J. Katz and associates, *No Time for Youth: Growth and Constraint in College Students* (San Francisco: Jossey-Bass, 1968), p. 76.
[2] Madison, pp. 128–129.

Students give other reasons that brought them to college, reasons that seem to make sense in terms of their own life style, but not reasons that college teachers seem to value. Quite a few see in college an opportunity to gain deeper insight into their own identity. They bring with them strong vestigial remnants of childhood narcissism and excessive dependence on parents. They feel that getting away from home, relating to others, and exploring the great ideas will help them discover who they are and where they want to go. Other students come with the calculated idea of gaining occupational skills which will be immediately rewarding, and they do not really care about the nuances of academic discourse. Vague as their vocational goals may be, these students have assimilated the point of view prevailing in the culture: college is a place to gain occupational competence and college students are willing to exchange their time and money for those desirable skills.

Still others testify that they come to college because it is the thing to do. They come from professional or intellectual families in which it is simply assumed that children go to college, or they come from communities which exercise heavy pressures for members of some classes to attend college. Not a few regard college as a burdensome task necessary to gain the credentials for desired status in society. Women frequently attend college to find potential mates. In this regard, colleges seem to serve the role of "fatting houses," which in some primitive societies are places where girls of marriageable age are placed to signify that they are eligible for marriage and to screen out males who are not clearly eligible to be their mates.

A particularly serious student reflects on why he attended a highly selective institution:[3]

I was probably less concerned in the freshman year with the academic sort of things. I was more concerned with having a good time, with going out, getting drunk. . . . I always felt myself independent whether I was or not. The image really had nothing to do with reality. . . . When I first came, I had the confidence of ignorance. . . . Just coming to college is enough to make anyone lose their confidence. Now my confidence is starting to come

[3] J. Katz, "Four Years of Growth, Conflict, and Compliance," in Katz and associates, p. 10.

back. . . . The thing that I valued most was being in a position of power; being a leader, an organizer.

Although students may appear poised and self-possessed to the middle-aged person, they testify that they are far from it. They are seeking not merely the appearance but the substance of self-confidence. And they appear to experience trauma when the conduct of courses and the comportment of professors seem deliberately designed to impair their self-confidence and poise. They are inclined to steer away from close contact with others because they feel awkward in establishing such relationships. A number confess to complete inability to engage other students in serious conversation, although they would like to do so.

In anticipation of college and from actual experiences, students value personal relationships as among the most potent forces in their development. Illustrative is the testimony of students on an overseas experience shared by more than half of one institution's graduate student body. Students go to overseas centers in relatively small groups accompanied by a small cadre of their own professors, and they live in an environment of intimacy. When they return to the home campus, they maintain the friendships formed overseas, even when they live in widely different parts of the campus. It generally takes several terms for them to overcome the reliance they have placed on the overseas group.

It could be argued that it was the overseas experience which was telling, but other sorts of overseas programs have not had such impact. This example simply underscores the point that the peer group culture is of such significance that it can scarcely be overemphasized. Contemporary research reinforces some insights of earlier educators such as Woodrow Wilson, who believed that a college with limited resources should construct only a residence hall, which would allow students to instruct each other. Then, if funds were available a library might be a nice addition. He saved for low priority the construction of classroom facilities and the employment of a faculty.

In a recent study, students at two highly selective institutions said they believe that personal relationships contributed most to changes in themselves. Responses to all questions of relations with other people—in living groups, contact with a variety of people on campus, dating, love, and marriage—raised personal influences to well over half of all influences that contributed to changes. And, indicative of the earlier point, "next in order of frequency are responses in which the student reports his own inward disposition as a major source of change; his self-awareness, personal philosophy, self-reliance, and responsibility."[4]

In spite of publicized student concern for altruistic enterprises and involvement in political action, students participate much more actively in social and athletic activities than they do in humanitarian or artistic ones. The dynamics of this phenomenon are complex. Students in interviews indicate slight guilt feelings about activities in which they either actively or passively participate as somehow antithetical to the prevailing academic emphases which characterize their institutions. Yet they do participate in spite of those guilt feelings, even to the neglect of their academic concerns. Their preoccupation with social activities is not simply gregariousness, but rather "evidence of the deep concern students have with just getting closer to other people and establishing more satisfactory communication."[5]

Students in the 1950s and 1960s for the most part rejected the large, somewhat formal social activity in favor of small, intimate group activity. The Saturday night phenomenon of several couples gathering in one apartment to prepare meals, listen to records, and engage in conversation seems reasonably typical. This need for closer communication with others is an element which runs through much of student commentary. College seniors reflecting on their four years' experience reveal again that relations with other people are of paramount importance to them. "They feel that they have made progress in their relations with others, and at the same time feel troubled that they have not come as close to other people as they desired."[6]

This desire for closeness is apparent in sexual relationships. Students appear much more open in conversation about sexual matters than did college students in the forties or earlier, although

[4] Katz, p. 13.
[5] Katz, p. 69.
[6] Katz, p. 69.

the evidence about actual sexual behavior is inconclusive and does not support the idea of a revolution in sexual behavior. The evidence does support the belief that students in the 1970s view sexual behavior as a means of getting close to others rather than as an exclusively erotic preoccupation.

Whether students attend highly selective institutions and are somewhat conservative in their political behavior or whether they are militant leftists, this element of close friendship strongly appeals to them. Contrary to expectations and to folklore, a relatively high proportion of college students do not date or date infrequently. Part of this seems to stem from an unsureness about themselves and how to go about the process of mate selection. One student who participated in Viet Nam Summer could almost serve as a spokesman for his generation:[7]

So I went to college, and college meant I was living with people, other people my age. The atmosphere was very liberal . . . but for a year I went around being very rigid. . . . I didn't have very many friends other than the political ones. We formed ourselves a little clique. . . . We didn't involve other people in decision-making at all. But I sort of gradually changed. I made new friends in the second year. I got two new roommates that I was very close to. You know, I made a lot of close friends. That really helped me out a lot. I didn't change my basic politics, but the experience just helped me personally. I think that you can't have very strong political ideas or do a lot of political things without that interacting with your personality.

Students, then, are forced to make important decisions with very little realistic information and few of the skills needed to fashion wise decisions. They are inclined to drift into the selection of a major and a vocation and frequently encounter serious problems in trying to live up to a commitment for which they are unprepared. Undoubtedly, family aspirations are involved. The young girl who identified strongly with her intellectual father set high political office as an initial goal, only to find that this conflicted with other emerging facets of her personality. When the conflicts intensified, the qual-

[7] K. Keniston, *Young Radicals* (New York: Harcourt Brace Jovanovich, 1968), pp. 90–91.

ity of her academic work dropped and her anxiety and frustration rose.

Students are demanding a great deal more information and consultation early in their college careers on the choice of a major and a career. Women students, especially in highly selective institutions, face even more serious conflict. At institutions that send from 70 to 90 per cent of their graduates to graduate and professional schools women students are strongly drawn toward the life of a professional intellectual, yet they sometimes consciously see the role of wife and mother as their primary goal. The conflict between these two aspirations seems generally dramatic and hurtful, and many women just drift into a resolution. A senior student reveals these crosscurrents in her reflections: [8]

When I first came here, I thought that when I was my present age I would not be thinking about marriage; that I would not be relating my goals or future plans to any other person. I thought that it was unwise; that it was wrong—not in a moral sense, but a mistake. I thought this because this is what my father told me for a long time. And, I believe it; I really do. I think it is a mistake, and I would teach my children the same thing. But I am doing it now.

Well, this is actually . . . a personal conflict. Since I was in high school, I have always wanted to get a bachelor's degree and then get a master's. Then do something either with the government, such as the information agency, or in the foreign branch of some kind of private institution, such as a corporation. This is what I want to do, ideally. However, I would have to admit that [now] Neil enters in. In a way, I am really sorry that I have met Neil as early as I have because . . . if it came to choosing between someone I really liked and getting a job, I think I probably would get married. But yet, it would be so much easier if I didn't have to make any decision like this. If there was not a complication of having someone I might possibly marry, this [working with the government] is what I would ideally like to do. But now, I don't know how it would be modified. It's too early to say.

[8] Madison, pp. 136–137.

Students assign scant importance to the curriculum. Less than one-fourth of the students at Berkeley and Stanford appear to have any intrinsic involvement with their courses in the formal curriculum. At Antioch College, less than 20 per cent of one senior class listed its courses or the instruction it received among the strong influences shaping its development. Keniston talks about the backgrounds of young radicals:[9]

Almost all reported little difficulty in doing outstanding work in high school and college, but despite academic success most of these young men and women became increasingly disregardful of formal academic requirements and more and more dubious about the value of academic performances per se. One young radical said, for example: "I went through college with a fair amount of ease. I never studied. I could always get by without studying and play around a lot. I didn't take school that seriously. I never thought you had to study to get a lot out of it. If I had a professor who I didn't like or who I thought was a poor professor, I wouldn't study for him and would get a C and it wouldn't bother me. But if I had a professor I liked and thought was a good teacher, then I would work very hard for him. . . . I always felt that the people who really studied hard were kind of dull people. I would see them getting into a box of not being really creative at all. I think they'd just be studying a lot and not learning anything."

Students are generally strongly bent on getting good grades, thus reinforcing the generalization that grades are the single most important motivation for academic work. Yet students attach little importance to getting to know their professors personally either in or out of class. Nor do students generally see professors as very influential in their lives. Yet at the same time students seem to search for a parent surrogate to whom they can transfer their feelings for their own fathers and with whom they can identify. Students are searching for appropriate role models from among the professoriate, but at the same time they don't feel compelled to be intimately involved with many professors. A female student would like to be like Professor Blank, who was in China during World War II and who

[9] Keniston, p. 89.

formulated a lot of American foreign policy. She realizes that no one could ever go back and do the same thing, yet she would like to be as he is. Such comments appear frequently in student testimony, but are always juxtaposed with other comments assigning even greater value to friends among the student peer group.

In the American tradition of adolescence there is a turning away from the family and from authority figures to peer group culture and an acceptance of its norms as infallible and regulatory. However, there is the countervailing need ultimately to find appropriate role models, and apparently American higher education has not consciously provided its students with much help in this.

Students of all sorts and at all institutions are caustic in their distaste for college housing. While residence hall design is gradually changing, the typical residence hall seems almost deliberately contrived to deny students privacy or a chance to function socially. The long corridors lined with cell blocks of rooms, each of which contains two or three students, stand in stark contrast to the sort of living arrangements middle class students in the 1970s experienced at home before they reached college. They find the arrangements an outrage against their need for privacy and amenities and as quickly as regulations permit, they move off-campus into apartments or rooming houses in which students can form small intimate groups. While many students, especially girls urged by their parents, happily enter a residence hall or sorority house their freshman year, they find that by the end of the first semester their need for that particular security has disappeared and they seek a much smaller and more primary style of group living.

This distaste for residence hall living suggests that students almost intuitively feel certain needs which must be satisfied if they are to achieve optimal development. In a highly structured residence hall unit, they must repress their emotions behind an even more rigid mask than they are forced to wear in their classes. They want freedom for impulse expression which can come about in a smaller group manifesting mutual trust and respect. They can't find this freedom in dealing with their professors, in student government, or in other formal kinds of campus activities. Hence, they search for it in less formal living arrangements.

Evidence from several sources stresses the need of under-graduate students for more freedom, both intellectual and personal, than it has been customary for colleges to grant. Creative college students almost demand the opportunity to be independent and innovative. They say that the further they go in college the more restrictive they feel academic requirements are. A creative student with a reasonably apparent talent in some field wishes to immerse himself in activities encouraging the development of his talent, and he finds the requirements outside of his interest virtually meaningless.

Radical students make the same point. At an early age they begin to feel restive with requirements and regulations based on rea-sons they cannot comprehend. Indeed, one of the reasons students move into radical causes is to find the freedom to involve themselves deeply in a subject. They almost intuitively decide that personal development requires deep personal involvement in something. More average students make the same claim. They tolerate requirements and, to them, excessive numbers of courses for the sake of the de-gree; but they generally don't involve themselves in more than one or two course activities. They select these in the light of their own developmental needs rather than the needs posited by faculty com-mittees or departments.

Students in professional schools make similar choices. Becker showed, for example, that medical students would extract from the curriculum those things which they believed would most facilitate their own entry into the practice of a profession.[10] Thus, the aspiring pediatrician, psychiatrist, or internist treats gross anatomy quite lightly and copies analyses from the notebooks of fellow students aspiring to surgery rather than go into the cadaver himself. The psychiatrist, knowing that never in his professional career would he need to cut into human flesh and trace nerve endings, sees no reason why he should do it as a student. It is difficult to appraise practically these demands for greater freedom. In part, they may be artificial, representing no more than symbolic revolt against a substitute parental authority. But so strongly worded are student statements

[10] H. Becker and others, *Boys in White* (Chicago: University of Chicago Press, 1961).

against the oppressiveness of certain kinds of curriculum requirements that one is led to the conviction that colleges and universities
have been overly prescriptive.

Once again, current research seems to corroborate insights
of an earlier time. Charles Eliot, in his arguments for a free election
system, anticipated the arguments for freedom to make mistakes
which students in the 1970s are advancing. These ideas, separated
by generations, are so parallel that it may be well to recapitulate
Eliot's ideas: [11]

*For him, the prescribed curriculum meant routine learning and
routine teaching. It produced only an average product, "A gregar-
ious enthusiasm and a unanimous motive." By way of contrast with
this, the elective system awakened individual interest and, in so doing, resulted in harder, better work. Thus, the whole burden of motivation was shifted from external to internal compulsion. The student's own moral autonomy was developed. This, in Eliot's view,
was the only way in which the effective leaders of the future could
be trained. They could only be produced in an atmosphere of freedom. . . . Eliot always saw the elective plan as a true "system,"
not a "wide-open miscellaneous bazaar." . . . It presupposed a
"well-ordered series of consecutive courses in each large subject of
instruction," but he shied away from purposefully arranging electives
in groups. Groups of studies, he wrote, were "like ready-made
clothing, cut in regular sizes; they never fit any concrete individual."*

Compare these with 1968 statements by creative students.
Most of these students found their on-campus experience, especially
in their last years, to be "a pretty confining grind." One refers to a
"deadly routine" in which the upperclassmen traveled in narrower
and narrower channels. None of the interviewees speak of any
novelty, challenge, or aesthetic stimulation in the last years' programs. Some students beat the mundane routine by noncurricular
involvements, but generally at a cost to their course work and grades.
Several students indicate that they lacked opportunities to participate in the wealth of living and the excitement of learning things of

[11] J. S. Brubacher and W. Rudy, *Higher Education in Transition*
(New York: Harper and Row, 1958), p. 109.

personal interest. To them, college education seemed an enforced detour which kept them from essential perceptual and emotional satisfactions.[12]

Particularly troublesome to interpret are conflict and anxiety among students in highly selective institutions. It appears that high achievement and high rates of development involve a great deal of personal conflict. Among creative students there appear consistently a high level of personal anxiety and major efforts to cope with and live with anxiety. When highly creative individuals are studied in detail, they uniformly testify to great anxiety, even to the point of physical reaction, either just before or during the creative act. Radical students describe immense personal turmoil as they decide to move against the prevailing currents of society. The dynamics of this phenomenon are little understood, but it does appear that conflict, anxiety, and tension at some level are essential for personal development. Whether an institution should deliberately contrive tension-producing situations is moot; what is clear is that institutions must accept a great deal of tension among students—even when it results in outbursts against the system—as essential for personal development. The college years may not be a particularly euphoric time, but ideally ought to be a satisfying time during which students encounter tensions and anxieties within themselves and learn to put them to the service of the developing personality.

Students seem to have sensed a fundamental change in life style in the United States more readily than have their professors or their parents. Institutions have failed to recognize that in many respects college students today represent a new kind of adolescence requiring a special kind of response. It is also true, of course, that students have been reluctant to face the fact that they are still not adults in the full sense of that concept.

We can define adolescence as that period between childhood and responsibility for one's self, mate, children, and society. It is, to be sure, a biological phenomenon entailing the advent of puberty; but it is also a cultural crisis of both status and function. Within American middle-class society there has always been some dysfunction between adult prerogatives and adult functions. One may drive

[12] P. Heist (Ed.), *The Creative College Student: An Unmet Challenge* (San Francisco: Jossey-Bass, 1968).

a car at sixteen, kill at eighteen, drink at twenty-one—all adult acts—but one cannot function as an adult in economic self-sufficiency until around the age of twenty-five. In the past, biological and functioning adulthood were achieved within a short span of time. Puberty came between twelve and fourteen, the end of school at sixteen or eighteen, marriage at nineteen or twenty, franchise at twenty-one, and a full-time job at about the same time. During that five-year period, the characteristics of self-consciousness, exclusive allegiance to peer groups, irresponsible criticism of adult values, and the hiatus state (neither child nor adult) could be tolerated and ways worked out within the family to contain extreme manifestations.

At present, however, a number of forces extend the period of cultural adolescence. The very young teenager has achieved economic power, yet in his late twenties still may not be economically responsible for himself. Puberty may come slightly earlier, and the opportunities for killing or marrying occur more frequently, but formally ending education comes a great deal later. The time span of incomplete adulthood has been extended from perhaps five years to ten or fifteen years. At the same time, institutions other than the family, church, and high school are required to deal with many adolescents. Thus the contemporary university is faced with finding ways of dealing with large numbers of students who have achieved biological and other prerogatives of adulthood, yet who cannot really be responsible for themselves, their mates, their children, or society in any but limited ways. Students seem sincerely in search of ways to handle this ambivalent role and are asking the curriculum for insights and their professors for understanding.

These observations can be quickly summarized. College students seek ways to expand their impulse life to use powers of affection or emotion for total personal development. They demand ways to explore in ways consistent to them, and are inclined to decry the "rat race" of prerequisites and too many courses. Although they get their greatest satisfactions from the peer group culture and are searching for ways to make themselves independent of their families, they nonetheless search for adequate and appropriate adult role models with whom to identify or test their own emerging feelings of personal identity. Especially do they look to these role models for help as they move into full adult status. Perhaps the most common goal students choose is greater self-understanding and greater awareness of their own identities. They sense that to move toward greater self-understanding they must find greater group identification and more powerful ways of relating intimately with other people. Here, students are inclined to use social or athletic activities as better devices for personal development than the formal curriculum or intimate contact with many teachers.

The developmental period spanning the college years appears to be a tension and anxiety-laden time, but students do not feel that this need be especially debilitating. They recognize the pain of conflict and would like assistance on their terms in resolving it; they do not judge it as catastrophic. Generally, students do not view the college curriculum as particularly pertinent to them, nor is it judged retrospectively as having made much contribution to their personal development.

Different sorts of students reject the curriculum for different sorts of reasons. Creative students find that it keeps them from deep immersion in the varieties of expression appropriate for their talent. Radical students find that the curriculum does not touch the deep problems of society which they view. Female students find that the curriculum intensifies their own struggle for appropriate role models; and black students testify that the curriculum is geared to a white middle-class society and is quite irrelevant to the feelings and needs of Negro students. Students who drop out of college for reasons other than manifest lack of ability to cope with the curriculum say that their courses simply do not speak to their perceived concerns.

In addition to consistent findings on the needs and desires of college students in general, there is an emerging collection of observations and hypotheses on the minority who engage in protests of various sorts. Some of the observations may be distorted and some hypotheses will ultimately be rejected, but this material does provide important substance if it can be interpreted. Seymour L. Halleck, drawing largely on clinical material, has a number of definite hypotheses to account for student unrest.[13]

[13] S. L. Halleck, "Hypotheses about Student Unrest," *Today's Education,* 1968, *56* (6), 22–26.

Activist and alienated students who were interviewed relate to the adult generation with difficulty. Many are highly articulate, irreverent, humorless, and relentless in their contempt for what they see as adult hypocrisy. They are highly peer-oriented; their peers rather than their parents shape their beliefs. One plausible explanation is that the present generation of students has been reared too permissively, that parents trying to understand their children have neglected to teach and discipline them, thus producing a generation of spoiled, greedy youth. Supporting this idea is the fact that activist and alienated students typically come from liberal, well-educated, professional homes where there is freedom to criticize and question. Frequently these children attended progressive schools. When they experience discipline, even rational forms of discipline, they tend to react with rage. When demands are not met immediately, they tend to withdraw or wrap themselves in a cloak of despair. Having come from psychologically sophisticated families, such students are likely to regard background factors as responsible for their aberrant behavior rather than to assume personal responsibility for it.

A related interpretation suggests that the alienated or restless student is a product of an affluent society in the sense that unearned affluence generates restlessness, boredom, and meaninglessness. Having virtually everything they could desire, affluent youth cannot set goals for themselves. A third possibility is that restlessness derives from the troubled nature of the world in which the students of the 1960s and 1970s are growing up. It is a world divided into two military camps, and his own camp needs the student's highly developed skills to win the war, cold or hot. Thus, students have been force-fed intellectually and they frequently arrive at college partially burned out. Students generally come to view this ceaseless competition as a form of paranoia fostered by a university which has become an arm of the government. These feelings are intensified by the war in Viet Nam and its attendant brutality and inequities.

The draft is a particularly villainous element. It leaves students uncertain about their future and students appear to carry a heavy load of guilt over the fact that they are in college rather than in Viet Nam. Many students also respond to the deterioration of the quality of life across the nation. Overpopulation, the pollution of resources, and the painful anonymity of bigness make the overcrowded campuses a particularly appropriate target. The problems appear to be of such magnitude that students become convinced that solutions cannot be found through the existing system. Another major malfunction of society which is intrinsically involved in student protest is the civil rights movement and the commitment to the cause of the Negro American. Not only did the movement show students the worst features of American life, but it also developed in them the skills of protest through passive, nonviolent sit-ins and the like.

Still another explanation of student behavior is that they are struggling to find new roles of psychological adaptation to a society which is massively, rapidly, and qualitatively changing. The sheer rate of technological change makes it impossible to predict what life will be like ten years from now; no one knows what values will be viable in a society that cannot be envisioned. If the future cannot be foretold, the argument goes, the wise course is to live existentially in the present.

In a sense, the psychological impact of television has been as profound as that of any recent technological advance. One reason is that television brings unselectively the vast range of human problems to children before they are able to assimilate them. Television acquaints youth with the cynical facts of life at a time when those facts are simply indigestible. Knowledge is communicated so quickly that there is little opportunity to live with myth or self-delusion. The result has been that youth acquire a deep skepticism about the validity of authority that has been reinforced as the whole society has turned increasingly to science rather than religion for the answers to life's questions. (Kenneth Keniston advanced parallel but somewhat different interpretations of the problems and needs of youth in America.[14])

The sheer rapidity of technological and social change and the expectation of still more innovation affect self-concepts, visions of the future, and how one ties to the symbols of the past. Change has become so much a part of life that society seems to value scien-

[14] K. Keniston, "Social Change and Youth in America," in K. Yamamoto (Ed.), *The College Student and His Culture: An Analysis* (Boston: Houghton Mifflin, 1967).

tific innovation and technological change without conscious reservation.

Thus, in an unstable and changing world young people grow up with characteristics that are puzzling and disturbing to adults. Youth evidence no deep commitment to adult values and roles, for they see the world into which they are headed as cold, mechanical, abstract, specialized, and emotionally meaningless. They feel forced into detachment and premature cynicism because this changing society seems to offer little that is stable or promising. Subconsciously, students realize that the world of the future is so different from the one in which they grew up that there are no appropriate role models for their lives, so parents and teachers are judged increasingly useless as role models. This is not rebelliousness, for young people are not rebelling against parents or their generation. Rebellion presupposes that the target of hostility is an active threat, but the young see no threat, for they see no possibility that they will ever be like their parents. This is in no sense critical of parents for, as previously noted, parents of activist college students of the 1960s and 1970s are liberal, open, permissive, and should have been excellent models for their children. But in a time when the society is moving toward an unknown station, youth judges the lives and styles of parents as simply of no consequence.

Another affliction of rapid change is the widespread feeling of powerlessness. When the world is viewed as fluid and chaotic, individuals feel themselves victims of impersonal forces which they can seldom understand and never control. It is this feeling of impotence which seems to make students cynical about the values of work and discipline. If one is pessimistic about ever having the power to affect corporations, government, or universities, dropping out makes more sense than subjecting oneself to fruitless discipline. Since the larger society is seen as not being amenable to control or manipulation, young people retreat into small, manageable groups. Students seek intimate personal contact with peers because they can comprehend the significance of a touch, a voice, or a smile, whereas they cannot comprehend the mutations of the stock market or of foreign policy.

This feeling of powerlessness also seems to account for the decline of political action among college youth. While the press makes painfully clear that some young people are concerned about politics, youth are still underrepresented among registered voters, and even activist youth do not have a well-articulated program. Instead of being politically conscious, college students seem to have developed a cult of experience which places the highest value on the maximum possible number of sense experiences. These come from intimate personal interaction with others, from experimentation with drugs, and even from the unusual juxtaposition of fabrics in wearing apparel. This aimlessness is intensified by the fact that formalized rites of initiation into adulthood have been clouded over or removed completely. As noted earlier, adolescence has been so extended as to lose its critical significance as a turning point in life. It has almost become an intuitively discovered replacement for the lost rites of initiation. Youth have developed their own culture, not with the goal of socializing people into the larger society, but as a means for individuals to form their own identities without knowing ultimate adult roles they might fill.

American youth in the 1970s thus seem to be drifting away from public involvement and social responsibility and toward a world of private and personal satisfactions. It is impossible to tell the long-term importance of radical youth, but it is possible that radical youth will ultimately set the style for a full generation, and it is just possible that out of the concerns, needs, and desires of militant youth will come insights into how the college curriculum can be restructured.

Once again, Kenneth Keniston provides comments that express the feelings of radical students.[15]

One of the things I've learned about the last two years is that you don't need very much to live on. . . . The kind of people who get involved in the Movement are really people who have a strong need for friendship.

The politics came after the people. There was always a personal relationship first.

I don't have an ideology.

I've had a lot of help because you know there's motion in the Move-

[15] Keniston, *Young Radicals,* pp. 20–43.

ment. There are people doing things, there are things happening, there are all kinds of exciting people.

It just seems to me that what happened is that I saw a different way of relating to people.

That kind of thing was in the back of my mind nagging at me: "You're not involved, you're not doing anything."

I don't get upset about sexual things, and don't get upset about religious things. But I feel that honesty, among yourselves, is necessary. . . . If I let down all my defenses, I would wind up being Billy Graham or Elmer Gantry.

After you get back to your apartment, or wherever you live, you see how few you are, and it gets to be very discouraging.

I seem to be moving irrationally into that, using my parents' relationships as a model for my relationships with Judy. . . . That makes me very upset because I consider my father a failure.

I feel that I should read more, but I feel that I have worked so long and I'm so exhausted that I just can't.

I have developed very well certain abilities, really pushed them to the limit of their development at this stage of my life.

I'm looking forward to really try to explain to [my parents] the kind of thing I feel, that I am a very personal embodiment of what they are, what they created in a son, and what they brought me up to be.

There are very few academics who see some kind of relationship to what's happening in the world. I don't want to be a scholar, but at some point I feel a responsibility to bring education to bear on my world.

I don't see myself going into the academic world. . . . I don't think I would be happy in it. . . . I don't want to take a job where I would have to "operate." I just don't like to get the feeling that I'm all alone and I'm doing something to everybody else.

I don't know what I'm going to do. I don't think I want to be a full-time politico . . . and I don't see academics as the center of things. . . . On the other hand, I don't think I could become a truck driver. . . . And it's very important for me to live among people I can communicate with.

I escaped and got lost in reading, and I enjoyed it for a while. And then started listening to the radio, "Another fifty thousand troops going to Viet Nam," and I would say, "What the f - - - am I reading this for, I've got to get back into some group."

One thing that took me a long time to learn is that there are models of marriage and adult life but that they don't work.

How do you be an adult in this world?

One thing I found at school is that I never had much sympathy for executive life or suburban life.

Who knows what the Movement is going to be like in ten years?

I still feel very proud of the fact that I can cry, that things can really dig me up inside; that I can cry when I'm happy. [After an evening with a friend], I just went upstairs and my eyes filled up, I felt so good. I felt so turned on and I hadn't touched anything all evening. I got so high, so turned on, just being able to do that—it really digs me being able to be happy.

Out of such sentiments certain yearnings or needs emerge. Radical youth seek new forms of adulthood dedicated to the betterment of society but not requiring blind acceptance of the established system. They seek a new approach to the future which avoids fixed tasks and defined life works, a viewpoint which stresses means, not ends. They want new pathways of personal development which allow the openness of youth and its responsiveness to inner life to last throughout life. They want new values for living which fill the spiritual emptiness created by material affluence. They search for new styles of human interaction which allow participants to grow in dignity and strength, for they are repelled by the impersonality, cruelty, and dehumanization of modern transactions between people.

Youth want new ways of knowing which combine intense personal conversation with academic knowledge. They want new kinds of learning which maximize the involvement of the intellect with the individual's experience, rather than dividing the two. They search for new concepts of man in society which acknowledge the unique individuality of each human being, but which also stress social involvement. They seek new ways to apply the radicalism they have experienced. They search for new types of social organization which include rather than exclude certain groups (thus, the encompassing feeling toward Negroes). They look for a new tactic of political action which enhances the awareness of those who participate in it. They want new types of international relations which allow men of diverse nations to respect common humanity and cultural uniqueness. Above all, these radical students search for new controls on violence between man and man, society and society, nation and nation. This search has caused the emphasis on love in the lives of radical students.

Nonconforming students present still further evidence about the needs and desires of some students. As indicated in the Muscatine Report at Berkeley,[16] these students reject outright many aspects of present-day America, believing that society is controlled by a group which has abandoned the common welfare and has resorted to manipulating the general public. They sense hypocrisy in the claims the dominant group makes about freedom, religion, patriotism, and morality, and its condonation of slums, racial segregation, migrant farm workers, and false advertising. They feel that to succeed in society as it is, one must mask one's real feelings and become an "organization man." They are terrified by their belief that the failure of the individual sense of responsibility, combined with impersonalized technology and cybernation, is producing a bureaucratized, machine-run society They say that if man is to remain in the world at all he must halt the computers.

To these students the older and faulty generation is represented most clearly by their parents, who have accepted the system and made their way in it. They are inclined to judge the whole society decadent and the dominant intellectual traditions sterile. To these youth, the only valid intellectual or artistic statements are being made by folk singers, Negro musicians, and avant-garde artists and writers. These students are clearly in revolt against such traditional American ideals as the Puritan ethic, individualism, and old fashioned patriotism. They find individualism in the form of private

16 Select Committee, *Education at Berkeley* (Berkeley: University of California, 1964).

property evil when it justifies exorbitant wealth, dishonest products, and segregated housing. Against these, nonconforming students flaunt sexual and emotional freedom.

Although nonconforming students reject the system, they seem to have a high commitment to form and style. For example, in personal relations the highest form of style is being "cool," but playing it cool ultimately seems to deny satisfying personal relationships. So, in a search for genuine experience, students experiment with nonaddictive hallucinatory drugs in the hope that, once free from the shackles of reason and logic, they can apprehend truth and become truly creative. There is a desire for instant poetry, instant psychoanalysis, and instant mysticism. Although nonconforming students reject formal ideologies and openly admire anarchism and existentialism, they seldom act as individuals, preferring instead to form groups to organize public acts of protest, petitions, marches, vigils, sit-ins, and civil disobedience. To join a cause and to form a group is a means of alleviating loneliness and alienation which they experience in their lives. Nonconforming youth are impatient in their search for instant remedies for both public and private ills.[17] "The unconventional student is inordinately sure that his own picture of the world is the correct one. He lacks the perspective necessary for self-criticism and for an appreciation of his opponent's position."[18]

With respect to the university, the nonconforming student is caustic in his judgments and radical in his proposed remedies. He came to college expecting to discover a community, but he discovered that communication with the older generation failed to materialize and that few of his teachers even knew his name. He discovered that his worth was measured by performance on examinations, not on a personal assessment of his work and ideas. He discovered that professors have their own system and play their own game, in which research is a means for personal advancement rather than a search for truth. Although the student had hoped that the humanities and the social sciences might be more concerned with human conditions than the natural sciences, these hopes were dashed because the professor's fame derives from publications rather than teaching.

[17] Select Committee.
[18] Select Committee, p. 32.

*In sum, the dissatisfied student finds the university to be just an-
other part of the established order. His alienation from society turns
into an alienation from his university. His distrust for the older
generation makes it difficult for him to appreciate traditional
methods of instruction or the faculty's idea of a good education,
especially when some professors do in fact display insouciance in
their teaching. The student's view of the university is moulded to
a large extent by the same willingness to accept imperfection that
moulds his general views of our social system.*[19]

Underlying student needs, demands, and desires are several
critical factors. The first is the general affluence of middle-class
white America, existing as it does beside a tradition rooted in
Calvinism and the rejection of pleasure. Both adults and students in
American colleges display considerable guilt over "never having had
it so good." Restless students opt for the poverty of the dropout.
Faculty opt for extending the work day and week into times once
reserved for recreation. The student who can wear old clothes, eat
simple fare, and scorn the "fat cats" can ease the guilt that comes
from knowing he has had a life of luxury. The professor who flies
at night to avoid losing a day's work and carries his "own" work
into the weekend is coping with similar feelings.

This problem of affluence is intensified by the plight of
minority groups in America and by the war in Viet Nam. There is
more than a suspicion that at least part of our present affluence is
war-based. Hence, to enjoy affluence is to condone a war, the justice
of which is in considerable doubt. The protesting college student
may well be compensating for his knowledge that if a war-based
economy had not made his parents affluent he might be fighting the
war rather than attending college. He knows that police billy clubs
are safer than Viet Cong grenades.

The moral dilemma of affluent America over the plight of the
Negro is the most divisive force in society. The guilt and grief with
which white America mourned the death of Martin Luther King,
Jr., is illustrative of a subterranean feeling present before his death.
It is no accident that student protests derived from the civil rights

[19] Select Committee, p. 34.

movement. When that movement ceased to welcome white students, they used other protest activities to palliate the guilt of more than three hundred years of injustice.[20]

From student protest and aspiration we see that young men and women are floundering in a society that is disjointed by immense change and that they are disaffected with an economic system unconcerned with human welfare. We see that youth want more freedom, emotional experiences with their fellows, and learning which will fill their needs and educate them to cope with the alarmingly new and altering world about them. We see this new and demanding generation, but our institutions of higher learning appear to look the other way and treat them as if they were going into the world as it was before the conquest of outer space, the surfacing of profound problems of poverty and race, sexual liberation, an Asian war, and a cybernetic attack on individuality.

[20] L. B. Mayhew, "Changing the Balance of Power," *Saturday Review*, August 17, 1968, 48–49, 57–58.

III

College Structure
and
Faculty Power

We have suggested in previous chapters that the college curriculum has very little impact on the lives of college students. This lack of effect and consequent student dissent to the educational experiences they receive or fail to receive seems to come from the malfunction of elements of the organization and administration of American higher education.

Organization in American colleges and universities has for the most part developed incrementally from historical accidents. The primacy of the president and board of trustees seems to have evolved out of frontier conditions, where society did not include a large group of trained and respected professors. Instruction was carried on by tutors who were not presumed to have the ability or inclination to govern an institution. The department system for the control of curriculum and research, even in the undergraduate college, appears to be an import from the German university grafted onto the colonial undergraduate college. The expanded administrative bureaucracy, including titles assigned to positions, probably imitates organizational ideas of business corporations.

Such a patchwork structure functioned fairly well so long as individual institutions and the systems of higher education in America were relatively static and relatively unimportant in the economy and in the general organization of the society.

However, since the end of World War II the enormous expansion of research, the equally great increase in numbers of students, and the even greater escalation in cost of education put such stress on the old system of governance that institutions of higher education began to fail to deliver the educational services their clientele demanded. Close analysis of expressions of student discontent and of students' educational needs and demands reveals by implication a number of structural weaknesses or failings. These are emphasized because almost invariably, when an institution discovers serious curriculum failings, the fault is a malfunction of the administrative and organizational structure.

First among serious problems is the department system for the control of faculty appointment, curriculum, and, in pacesetting institutions, funding. Departments in large or small institutions seek to pattern themselves after prestigious, research-laden universities. In those institutions research and scholarship dictate staffing, and the curriculum is created to serve the research interests of faculty rather than the developmental needs of students. Large undergraduate enrollments in so-called service courses provide the subsidy for the smaller research-dominated seminars in the graduate school. The department is the bastion behind which faculty members can complete their professionalization and their own research and scholarly concerns. As outside funding for faculty research becomes available, the department can maintain a financial power balance with the institution. Through this independent financial power, the department can attract and maintain the loyalties of individual faculty members even at jeopardy to the institution as a whole.

This conflict of interest between the department and the institution is revealed by the differing views of federal support of higher education found within a given institution. Department chairmen are not much interested in direct institutional grants placed at the disposal of the central administration; they prefer instead the type of support which allocates funds to those departments able to mount successful research projects. Organisms resembling feudal baronies have arisen, with sufficient power to oppose any efforts of central administration to reform the educational mission of the university.

In one state college, for example, departments have gained such complete control over both permanent and part-time appointments that the nominal academic leaders of the institution are powerless to appoint people who have educational interests broader than promotion of the department discipline. The president of a Texas private institution almost in desperation created a separate university college, with its own dean and budget, to force departments to give attention to the educational needs of undergraduate students. The magnitude of his failure is demonstrated by the fact that within two years the university college had to content itself with part-time or underqualified staff, since the departments were unwilling to spare their senior scholars for service to undergraduate students. Clark Kerr outlines the severity of this matter when he judges that the university president is no longer a leader but rather is a mediator in the labor relations sense of the word.

An outgrowth and a cause of the department system is the reward system, which operates most visibly in complex, research-preoccupied institutions and which lesser breeds of institutions seek to emulate. This system, described by the aphorism "publish or perish," provides the rewards of status and well-being. Faculty members who are productive in research and conspicuous on the national academic and government scenes reap these rewards. Research contracts relieve professors of allegiance to their institutions, and consultation and participation in national organizations provide faculty members the security of knowing that if their interests are not met at one institution, they will be at another. In spite of lip service to the importance of teaching, publications, size of research contracts, and off-campus distinction rather than on-campus service to students (especially undergraduate students) determine promotions and salary raises.

"Any faculty member recommended for promotion exclusively on the basis of teaching ability will be automatically judged inadequate for this institution," said the chief academic officer of a major university. At the same university, at a meeting of full professors to consider promotions of colleagues, an individual well regarded for his skills as a teacher, his wisdom as a counselor, and his willingness to expend his energies in helping doctoral students with their dissertations was rejected for promotion because his list of publications was considered less than the norm established for that university.

In American colleges, graduate and professional schools were grafted onto the undergraduate college and, for a time, the demands for undergraduate education allowed these two styles of work to exist fairly peacefully together. However, particularly since World War II, which brought both increases in research funds and demands for graduate and professionally trained manpower, the graduate school has moved into ascendency. Teaching graduate students is more highly regarded than teaching undergraduate students, and the energies of senior professors are reserved for that work, leaving to less qualified persons the instruction of undergraduates, particularly in the first two years. So highly regarded is graduate teaching that something like one-third of the private liberal arts colleges in the United States offer graduate work so that they can compete with universities for new faculty members. Many a well-trained Ph.D. simply will not accept an appointment to teach only undergraduate students, since more money is spent on graduate instruction than on undergraduate instruction. Scarce resources are redirected from the service of undergraduates to graduate and postgraduate professional students.

Although not technically a matter of structure or organization, the system of professional ethics which governs the styles of American college professors is closely related to the role of scholar or research worker. There is scarcely a statement for the obligations of the professor as a helping professional seeking to encourage development of late-adolescent human beings. The concepts of academic freedom and permanent tenure are essentially artifacts

designed to give a professional worker in a hierarchical organization
entrepreneurial freedoms similar to those of the classic professions
of law and medicine. Under the existing system of ethics, the professor's "own work" is judged to be of greater significance than
service to his students.[1]

With these developments has evolved a bifurcated view of
human nature which holds that the intellectual side of a student is
of concern to professors, but all other facets of human personality
should properly be relegated to someone else. Two systems of administration have grown up: the dean of students and such subordinates
as counselors, directors of activities, and residence hall supervisors
concern themselves with matters other than those which preoccupy
professors, department heads, and academic deans. This system re-
places the concern with the total student which the colonial college
tutor or the pre-World War II liberal arts professor presumed to
be his proper job. We now have a cadre of specialists with no one
striving for fully integrated development of a maturing adult.

One institution tried to recreate the role of someone concerned with the academic interests and the personal problems of
students by organizing a group of faculty proctors, each of whom
would serve from twelve to fifteen students in a variety of professional capacities. Within a year of the inauguration of this system,
it became almost impossible to staff these faculty positions because
faculty members were willing to provide academic advice but were
unwilling to involve themselves in the personal needs of students.
Nor were faculty members willing to tolerate student personnel
officers providing academic advisement. As stated earlier, student
testimony indicates that they seek a mature adult professional with
whom they can discuss their concerns during the developmental
college years. Yet they find no one within the college structure who
is willing to assume such a role.

These generalizations do not apply to all institutions. Several
of the so-called experimental institutions, such as Bennington
College, Sarah Lawrence College, and Stephens College, have his-

---

[1] The reader interested in a more exhaustive treatment of this
theme is referred to a recent work by the senior author: L. B. Mayhew,
Arrogance on Campus (San Francisco: Jossey-Bass, 1970).

torically maintained the integrity of counseling in both academic and nonacademic matters. These institutions seem to have exerted a tremendous impact on the lives of their students. But, as a rule, bifurcation rather than integration characterizes most institutions.

The admission process, particularly with the growing scarcity of space in colleges, emphasizes a distorted view of human ability and exerts a generally unhealthy pressure on students, their parents, and the institutions themselves. As long as there was room for all who wished to attend college, institutions used the simple criterion of whether the student had the intellectual and character traits needed to survive. As competition for space increased, however, institutions became more selective, demanding high academic aptitude established by prior performance in secondary schools and by tests designed to measure this abstraction. High school students then began to bend their efforts not to full human development but to successful performance on the scholastic aptitude test and to clear demonstration that they had taken "solid subjects" in high school rather than those which conceivably could have added cubits to their total development. This drift toward high selectivity enables some institutions to limit enrollment to students graduating in the upper 1 to 5 percent of a high school graduating class, and smaller, less competitive institutions are following their example.

There is no evidence, however, that the top 1 or 5 per cent of high school graduates, as determined by academic performance, are more likely to develop into good human beings than those who perform at lower levels. Indeed, it seems likely that institutions are screening out highly productive humans without whose services society is substantially poorer. The three twentieth century American presidents who graduated from Harvard University would probably be barred from entry to that institution by standards of admission imposed in the 1960s.

The logical outcome of this selectivity is that each level of education has become more of a screening process or a hurdle to be overcome than a feasible and compatible program of education geared to humans at a given stage in their development. Thus, high school performance of a high level is valued primarily to safeguard entry into the proper college, undergraduate achievement is inspired

by the requirements of the graduate school, and graduate school
performance is dominated by the desire to enter a profession at the
highest status possible.

This high selectivity is manifest in the grading system. Grades
determine subsequent status in various levels of schooling; hence,
students devote their energies to securing high grades.[2] Even when
institutions allow some pass-fail work, students are inclined to exert
most effort in courses requiring grades, for it is the number of A's
which really pays off. Illustrative is an experiment at Ohio University called programed instruction, which allowed students to
accelerate work in either education or engineering. Students who
earned a grade of B were not allowed to raise that grade, so academically capable students would refuse the opportunities to accelerate simply in order to insure that the final grade was an A. The
preoccupation with grades would not be bad if it could be established that grades do measure important outcomes of education, but
grades seem primarily predictive of future grades. Thus the certify-
ing function of colleges and universities has developed a malignancy
—a preoccupation with letter grades. It is against this malignancy
that some of the most potent student protest has been directed.

Although other organizational weaknesses and failings are
relevant to the curriculum—the split in management of residence
halls between the business side and the program side; the increasing
impersonality of the registration process, which leaves students feeling as though they were IBM cards; the rise in tuition without a
noticeable increase in services to undergraduates; and the like—only
one further malfunction need be described in detail to outline the
parameters of the problem: the failure of educational leadership.

In earlier times, the president was responsible for exerting
educational leadership and for encouraging innovation. Historically
important innovations such as the free election system, lecture and
seminar instruction, and programs of general education were products of fertile presidential minds. As institutions become complex,
however, presidential energies have been directed to matters other
than education. Increasingly, presidents of large and small institu-

2 H. S. Becker and others, *Making the Grade* (New York: Wiley,
1968).

tions must spend much of their time off-campus raising funds from private and legislative sources, cultivating philanthropic and federal contacts, and attending to the investments and physical plant expansion of multimillion-dollar corporations.

Thus far, no other agency has appeared with the power or concern to exert consistent educational leadership. Faculty members, operating through departments, take much too narrow a view for broad leadership; board members can spend only a limited number of days on educational concerns; and the president is preoccupied elsewhere. Until new leadership arises, it is not likely that any broad-scale curriculum reform will take place.

It is apparent that a revised administrative and organizational structure for institutions of higher education is essential for curriculum reform. It is possible to visualize revised structures if some principles and guidelines can be developed. In one sense, the obverse of the weaknesses just noted can serve as guidelines: some agency must assume responsibility for broad educational leadership; the drift toward departmentalism and preoccupation with graduate education must be checked if the needs of undergraduate students are to be accommodated; and some less pressure-laden techniques for admission and assessment must be found if a healthy educational climate is to exist.

Several other guidelines suggest themselves. The college system must place the student and his needs first rather than focusing on academic subjects. The point of view must be developed that subjects in the undergraduate curriculum are simply techniques or instruments to facilitate human development rather than things of intrinsic worth themselves. Students testify that the curriculum as it presently operates is not relevant, nor does it facilitate their personal growth and development. Yet the curriculum is the resource upon which the institution relies to accomplish its educational mission. Not only should the student and his needs be the primary aim, but curricula should be sufficiently flexible to accommodate the multiplicity of needs of thousands of individual students. We noted earlier the dream of James Madison Woods, who believed that for a school of two thousand students there should be two thousand curricula, each tailored to the unique needs of an individual human being. Charles Eliot argued that the free election system was seeking the same end, relying on each student to select from a variety of offerings those elements he most required. However, the free election system left out an essential ingredient—adequate counseling to help students make reasonable choices.

Also necessary is an organization which is free enough to allow people to succeed and to fail. The entire range of activities—regularly scheduled classes, frequently administered tests, definitely prescribed prerequisites, class attendance policies, and other academic requirements—exist to ensure against possible failure. The potentiality of personal failure, and the fact that human beings develop in part as a result of facing tension and conflict, needs to be accepted.

College professors possess a wide range of highly developed talents which could be of enormous benefit to students if those talents were offered in ways which make sense to students. Unfortunately, because of departmentalism and preoccupation with subjects, professors are encouraged to expose their talents on their own terms rather than on those of students. Thus, it is convenient for a professor of history to meet a class three hours a week and demonstrate his expertise. But reasonably sophisticated college students can obtain information much more efficiently by reading a book, and a more profitable approach for many students would involve freedom to go to the professor only when they needed particular assistance.

Professors have adopted their style of behavior in response to their own personal needs. The professor lecturing about a subject which interests him is satisfying himself, as is the professor who visualizes himself as a master and his students as disciples. The professor who seeks to dominate a class from the lecture podium and the professor who gains a paternalistic pleasure from addressing students by their first names also are revealing basic individual needs. These needs must be recognized and accommodated, but satisfaction of professorial needs may be antithetical to the equally valid needs of students. If professors are to serve as members of a helping profession, some of their own needs must be sacrificed, with some form of compensation for this sacrifice.

One possible way of helping professors contribute constructively to students' education is to provide parallel systems of administration. One system would continue its present management function, setting institutional goals and maintaining normative standards, while the other would be available to render help, without sanction or appraisal, to faculty members who needed it. A dean could help professors to perfect goals and proposals, listen as the faculty member probes his own personal problems, or provide assistance on how to relate to students as the professor assumed a new and unfamiliar role.

Also needed is a reward system which can differentiate among the various interests and skills of professors. Not all professors are great or even adequate lecturers, yet the present system of organization almost requires lecturing because all faculty members hold teaching appointments. Not all professors have research talent, yet the present reward system places a premium on publications, no matter how poor. A pluralistic reward structure must be developed within an institution so that the talented lecturer, counselor, scholar, discussion leader, or consultant may be valued for his own unique contributions. Until such a system is devised, professors with no sense of writing style will feel constrained to write, no matter how tortuously; and professors ideally suited to be tutors will feel constrained to conserve their own time through formal lectures.

With the drift toward professionalization of faculty members and with the focus on subjects or disciplines rather than on the helping mission, we need a system which protects people against themselves. Bureaucratic structures and procedures could retard or block tendencies springing from the subject-matter professionalization of faculty members. A limit on the number of courses a department can offer could slow the proliferation of courses beyond the needs of undergraduate students. Requiring a periodic wholesale review and revision of the curriculum could prevent the entrenchment of archaic offerings. Roadblocks could make the all too common transition of a course from independent study to study in groups to formal organization much more difficult. The Bill of Rights of the U.S. Constitution was created in part to protect people against the oppressive and lethal expansion of quite human tendencies. Oppressive and lethal academic tendencies must also be exposed and suitable procedures created to minimize them.

Because primary group relationships seem so important to

student development, a system which will provide for groupings of smaller numbers of students is necessary. We frequently assume that department majors form a subculture of value to individuals, but this does not seem to hold true for undergraduates, especially those in large, complex institutions. Whether a revised grouping of students takes the form of a team-teaching subgroup, a cluster college, or a small association of freshmen, sophomores, juniors, and seniors will depend upon the history and tradition of the institution. The point is, the organizational structure must provide for these groupings regardless of the inconvenience to the institution's bureaucracy.

Colleges and universities have begun to accumulate considerable information about students—high school records, admission test scores, placement test scores, clinical judgments about individual students, and academic achievement data of various sorts. Some of this information approaches the validity and reliability of information obtained about medical patients. For example, some attitude test scores are more reliable than standard measures of blood pressure, and the potentialities of more refined diagnostic and prognostic measures are already visible. Yet professors typically do not use existing information in dealing with individual students. Professors rarely seek out placement test scores and the like, either because of their own disinclination to use them, or because the specialists, suspicious of possible misuse, will not allow professors access to these data. If the undergraduate college is truly to be a source of professional help to undergraduate students, it must provide easy access to data on individual students. Unless organization is improved through better record-keeping and dissemination of information about students to faculty members, it seems fruitless to accumulate more data.

Another kind of intelligence is needed, such as that in the entrepreneurial professions like law, medicine, and dentistry—the views of the clients are made known as they seek or reject the service of the practitioner. The college professor, however, is protected in his institutional setting against the operation of such a free market. Students attend his institution because of proximity, cost, family loyalty, or because a particular program is offered. Once enrolled, the student becomes a captive client for whatever practitioners the institution wishes to expose him to. An administrative system must be devised which will establish clear and open channels so that the opinions of the clients (students) are regularly and pointedly brought to the attention of the practitioner (professor). This will not be accomplished unless the administration provides for it and solicitation of client opinion becomes normal conduct.

Students require individual attention to their personal concerns from some professional person. Yet the way professorial resources are deployed, personal attention is almost precluded. Consider an institution of eight thousand students, with the tradition that the personal concerns of students are the responsibility of the twenty counselors in the counseling center—more than perfunctory attention to a few students is impossible.

A few institutions have developed different ways of deploying faculty resources. It is standard practice at Stephens College, for example, for every faculty member and professional administrator to assume counseling responsibilities for a group of eight to twelve students. Each adviser is expected to deal with academic, career, and emotional problems, and he has training to qualify him to do so. This arrangement rests on the principle that the student-faculty ratio, which runs from nine-to-one to twenty-to-one, provides an opportunity for personal interaction between students and faculty members.

Some of these suggestions for a more efficient and flexible administration and organization are realistic, while others might seem Utopian. None can be achieved, however, until a number of issues are resolved. The first issue relates to the purposes of the undergraduate college.

Several viewpoints oppose the establishment or reestablishment of goals for the undergraduate college. One, enunciated by Jacques Barzun, holds that the undergraduate college is either dead or dying, with its previous functions now performed by the secondary schools or the graduate schools. Another view holds that the essential role of the undergraduate college is to prepare students for graduate training or postbaccalaureate professional training. However, the realities of American life, which include an extension of preadult school life to the middle or late twenties, and the developmental needs of the people in the age group attending college, suggest that some formal educational effort should be made specifically for that age group. The seventeen- or eighteen-year-old is well on his way toward sociological or biological adulthood and is striving toward psychological and economic adulthod. He is in the process of discovering his emerging adult identity and developing his full cognitive and emotional powers. He is making crucial decisions which will determine his total adult development, and he needs help in doing so. If an institution recognizes the validity of such assistance to him, there are curriculum, instruction, and advising techniques available to achieve this goal.

For an institution to accept such a goal will mean rejecting other possible uses of resources. The predominantly undergraduate institution will refrain from extensive involvement in graduate training or continuing education if it is serious in its claim to make its undergraduate effort effective. The undergraduate colleges of complex institutions will deny the primary goal of feeding students into their own graduate and professional schools. Rather, they should let that flow happen almost as a serendipity derivative of rich undergraduate experience.

The issue of the professionalization of faculty must be faced and dealt with if the needs of the undergraduate students are to be met. The post-World War II climate has allowed faculties, particularly in complex, prestigious institutions, to become so professionalized as to approach syndicalism—the needs and ambitions of the members of the guild take precedence over all other concerns. The professoriate has become self-selecting, self-evaluating, and self-directing, and the professor's activities and priorities have increasingly been his own research, consulting, or service efforts. Professionalization in a broad sense of the word can be desirable, but in the undergraduate college the professionalization should concentrate on the needs and desires of undergraduate students. The ethics and the socialization within the profession, as has been previously stressed, also should be determined by that focus. The interests and needs of students approximate much more closely the concerns of administrators than the concerns of faculty. For a curriculum to be created with the needs of students in mind, this tendency should be modified so that the administration and faculty are equally concerned with the development of late-adolescent students.

A third issue is faculty autonomy. An argument can be

advanced that a professional faculty should be responsible for its own membership, the substance of the curriculum, the conditions of student entrance and exit at the institution, and broad policy regarding the general quality of student life. However, these prerogatives should be tempered by the prerogatives of other agencies, which take a broader view of the mission and goals of the institution. Some version of a corporate faculty, shared responsibility, and cooperative governance seems necessary, with financial authority and executive responsibility assigned to central administration. This arrangement, when properly used, stimulates creative faculty thought about its own membership and curricula. The issue becomes especially formidable when faculties seek more than shared responsibility and aspire to hegemony over the entire institution in order to exercise that authority for the furtherance of faculty interests. Perhaps this surge for complete control is a desire for compensation for decades during which central administration ruled institutions autocratically, arbitrarily, and without adequate recognition of the professional nature of professorial duties and responsibilities. Now, however, supreme administrative power has been terminated in all but limited numbers of junior colleges and church-related liberal arts colleges. To resolve the issue, effective ways must be found to equally curtail unbridled faculty power.

Another major issue calls for a definition of excellence. There can be no quarrel with the idea that every institution should aspire to excellence, but solid questions can be raised if every institution aspires to the same sort of excellence—an excellence characterized by increased selectivity and increased academic rigor in verbal and quantitative styles of reasoning. It should be possible for an institution to aim at the education of second- or third-chance students, and to do so as excellently as does the institution which concentrates on highly talented potential academicians. It should be possible for a junior college to strive for excellence in the training of technicians without feeling inferior to the medical school, which strives for similar levels of achievement in a different domain.

Unfortunately, when institutions do embark on a quest for excellence, they are likely to choose the limited concept. Emerging state colleges and state universities want to achieve the same sort of excellence that the senior state universities and private universities have achieved, with graduate and professional work and research representing success. When liberal arts colleges quest for excellence, they see its culmination in a high proportion of students who go on to graduate school, and in higher scholastic aptitude test scores of entering college students. David Riesman has characterized this upward mobility as a group of Avises seeking to become Hertzes. A more healthy metaphor would be for the Avises to strive to become outstanding Avises and nothing more.

IV

Status
Quo
Education

Higher education in the United States today is a major paradox. It is conducted in a society experiencing perhaps the most revolutionary changes in the history of mankind. Changes in medicine from the administration of antibiotics to the use of organ transplants have altered the whole concept of health. Changes in transportation, communication, agriculture, production, and scholarship have come with such rapidity that society has scarcely been able to adjust to them. Yet the processes and practices of college education have not changed appreciably since the middle of the nineteenth century, when the recitation technique gave way to the lecture, laboratory, and seminar methods of instruction.

One point of view could—and, we suspect, does—hold that the practices of higher education have been so effective that there is little reason to change them. But this view is scarcely consistent with the entire stance of society that change and improvement are possible and necessary. Further, it is not consistent with views and observations concerning teaching. Nowhere is the paradox of collegiate education so starkly revealed as in any examination of college teaching. College teachers see themselves, if one can believe what they say in essays, as possessing a mixture of virtues. In the view of one professor, the teacher becomes almost the personification of his subject, while another professor sees things in a somewhat different light:

Our task is to transform young, promising human beings into constructive, creative personalities who have realized themselves, who build their potentialities and achieve maturity as full as possible. The transformation of individual students into constructive, creative personalities is the end of teaching. Our work should focus on the student rather than on our discipline. On the student as a real flesh and blood, total human being there before us; on the student as an individual.[1]

Still another professor sees research involved:

The history of science is full of examples of great and small discoveries made by old and young scientists who have been looking for something. College teaching offers a wonderful opportunity to play this game of "seek and find." There are many problems which have puzzled scientists for many years. Goethe summed this all up when he said, "The greatest happiness that can come to a scientist is to explain the explainable and to patiently admire the inscrutable." Each new generation of young scientists gets its happiness by explaining in part what was inscrutable to the previous generation.[2]

From such opinions can be etched the picture of the college professor as the kindly mentor of youth who constantly brings to

[1] Unpublished letter to the senior author.
[2] R. G. Gustavson, *Discoveries Through Research: College Teaching as a Career* (Washington, D.C.: American Council on Education, 1958), p. 11.

the young the fresh insights which flow from his own scholarship, which he pursues in quiet contemplation. He is a thinking man who, by the virtues of his own life, serves as a model with which the best impulses of youth can identify. While on occasion he can be stern with students, it is always a sternness for growth, never for vindictive reasons.

Considerable substance supports this picture. There is the record of one distinguished professor who declined three presidencies and who wrote little so that he could remain with his students. Louis Agassiz could, by forcing students to attend to the detail of a dead fish, develop perceptive scientists. John Dewey, by the force of his intellect displayed in the lecture room, modified the thinking of a generation, which could then revolutionize the schools. And Mark Hopkins not only molded the thinking of those who came in contact with him, but he became the proof that his ideals of teaching could be realized.

This ideal vision, rooted though it may be in some reality, must be compared with another reality somewhat more spotted in character. Teachers generally are not really very important in the lives of students. Several thousand students in a social science course at Michigan State who completed an open-end questionnaire about important educational influences rarely, if ever, mentioned the teacher. Antioch College is generally regarded as an institution which has high impact on students, yet seniors there placed teaching and the curriculum quite low among the factors which influenced them during their college years. At the University of Tennessee, several studies of students who learned without class attendance suggested that in some courses students learn more by staying away from class than by having classroom contact with the teacher.

After visiting eighty different classes in nineteen selected colleges and universities, Dressel and Mayhew[3] concluded that, with a few notable exceptions, classes and courses in general education were routine lecture presentations of materials already available in textbooks, and that students did not appear to be particularly interested in what was being said. This lack of interest is typically manifested by letter-writing, sleeping, and reading from other text-

[3] P. Dressel and L. B. Mayhew, *General Education: Exploration in Evaluation* (Washington, D.C.: American Council on Education, 1954).

books during the lecture. Students' comments about teachers, obtained independently by both authors from nine different colleges during the past two years, also lead to this conclusion. Typical of student reactions are such statements as:

Teachers bore students with personal reminiscences, particularly of World War II experiences.

Teachers assign Mickey Mouse busy work.

While a few teachers meet student expectations, most do not and should be avoided.

Teachers cover the textbook in class, which seems a waste of time.

It is a myth that teachers like to be with students. They usually meet their classes, have coffee with other teachers, and then go home.

Teachers know their subjects, indeed, they are usually national authorities. Yet, they cannot seem to communicate with students.

A group of cadet teachers was asked to critically observe experienced teachers in various types of institutions. Although they were given no guidelines, they reported similar reactions: "Preoccupation with personal illustration." "Reading lecture notes." "Reading from the textbook." "Poor word selection." "Disturbing mannerisms." "Using arms rather than the blackboard to show a diagram." "Abdication of control of the class in the face of a two-student debate." Some bright spots were reported: one lecturer held a class spellbound for a full hour; another criticized student themes before the class without being hurtful even to those students whose papers were given grades of F; another presented an organized lecture which left the students feeling they had heard a high order of conversation. But of forty-five incidents reported spontaneously after observation, the large majority were severely criticized.

Further evidence on this matter of spotted reality is presented by some elements of the recent student protest movement. While many of the objects of student protest have to do with regulation of their private lives or moral dilemmas perplexing the entire society, some of the criticism about college education focuses on the kind of teaching students receive. Some students perceive the university to be a knowledge factory, forcing students either into large impersonal lectures or into discussion groups that are at the mercy of aspiring doctoral candidates who are more preoccupied with the progress of their dissertations than with the educational needs of students.

In the light of such evidence, the question that naturally arises is, Why is college teaching not changed? There seem to be a number of reasons, the most important of which is probably inertia —it is simply too difficult to change. It is much easier for a professor to use a lecture that is already prepared than to contrive new approaches. It is much easier to fall into an established pattern of classroom contact than to establish in behavioral terms the precise objectives of a course, a class, or other learning situation.

We have already alluded to the second barrier in a previous chapter—the way in which the reward system operates in higher education. Although institutions claim in their catalogs and their presidents claim in public speeches that teaching is a primary responsibility of colleges, the reward system does not support this contention. This is especially true in four-year institutions, which generally claim to value a merit system for promotion, tenure, and salary increases. Teaching is rarely considered except in the most haphazard and general way. Rather, those things which can be most easily quantified are considered.

Seemingly, something which can be counted, even at a very gross level, provides greater security than an attempt to assess such intangible things as classroom performance. Rewards are based on the quantification of such things as community service efforts, offices held in national societies, books or articles published, research grants, off-campus consultations, and research projects in progress. None of these has but the most tangential relationship to teaching. Further, even the quantification of these factors takes place at a gross and superficial level. For example, those who must judge generally simply count without ever reading the research publications the professor is supposed to have prepared.

A third barrier operates because so little is known about successful teaching. Even those who spend their lives thinking about successful teaching are not very convincing when they attempt to prove that they know what they are saying. Generalizations simply are not supported by good evidence; they become matters of opinion supported by rhetoric and logic, and to the disbeliever, this rhetoric is not very convincing. One educational psychologist, Ernest Hilgard, makes a pessimistic point: "Really, considering all the research which psychologists and educational psychologists have produced, there is precious little which has any relevance telling us how to do better this act of teaching. Outside of a few things, such as the laws of recency and primacy, and some notions of the value of reward and reinforcement, there are precious few things which the experimental psychologists have shown us which have relevance for how we conduct a class." [4]

This being so, and because so many experiments which do attempt to examine the dynamics of college teaching show no significant differences, the person who says, "If there are no significant differences, why rock the boat?" has powerful support. There is another stance one can take, however. Hilgard himself takes this view, saying that since in our experiments we come up with no significant differences, we can be reasonably sure that even with experimentation students are not too likely to be hurt significantly.[5] And it is just possible that from some experiments will come an approach which will reveal differences of genuine significance and statistical validity.

A fourth barrier to change in teaching practice involves a definite conflict of roles. Perhaps the biggest single problem American higher education has faced in the last one hundred years, and has so far failed to resolve, is the conflict between the research role of the university and its teaching function. In the United States, the contemporary institution is a complex marriage between the English-style undergraduate college and the German-style research university. There is the attempt to use the same faculty for both functions, and professors are struggling to resolve the resultant role conflict. There are perhaps twelve to fifteen hundred institutions in this country where the publish or perish policy is just not applicable and where it is nonsense to talk about such a matter. Yet even in those small liberal arts colleges, junior colleges, and teacher-prepara-

[4] E. R. Hilgard (paper delivered at the Fall Faculty Conference, Stephens College, Columbia, Mo., September 1965).
    [5] Hilgard.

tion institutions, faculties still act as though publish or perish were a reality. The explanation probably lies in the enormous influence the major universities have over the character of higher education, and the fact that teachers in other sorts of institutions undoubtedly took at least some of their graduate work in institutions in which the role conflict between researcher and teacher was real.

A related fact is that the product of a graduate school does not really know how to teach, nor is he prepared for teaching as an essential function. Some have had experience as teaching assistants, but this is routine work dealing with sections after the manner of the major professor. The majority have not had even that limited exposure. And the role model for the recent graduate is the major professor, whose first interests lie with his research and who regards teaching as the chore necessary to allow him his research time. The power as a role model of the major professor in graduate school has never been studied, but it is illustrated by two middle-aged professors who served at different universities. They were not at all physically similar, but they had a pronounced resemblance to each other. Their speech, mannerisms, vocabularies, and even gaits were alike. The explanation was that both had studied under a distinguished historian at the University of Michigan years before, and both had adopted their professor's style.

A fifth barrier to change in teaching practice is the fact that other changes have come about so rapidly. Institutions of higher education face problems today which ten years earlier were not problems. Take just one example, the private liberal arts college in which teaching is supposed to be the major preoccupation. There are approximately 850 institutions of this sort which up until the middle 1950s were quite small, simple institutions in which educational leadership could derive directly from the president.

But consider what has happened. In a scant eight to ten years, an institution previously having five to six hundred students, an operating budget of less than one million dollars, a physical plant which had experienced no additions for fifty years, and a president who could know personally every student and faculty member on campus, has grown to the size of twelve to fifteen hundred students. The faculty has doubled in size, the operating budget is now over four million dollars, new buildings are being constructed at the rate of a quarter of a million dollars' worth a year, and the president is on the road most of the time securing the necessary funds and support of an increasingly costly educational enterprise. In the middle 1950s the institution could get along quite nicely without an academic dean. Currently the president is perplexed about why he can no longer exert educational leadership.

This matter of change within colleges is so enormous that it should be elaborated still further. There is considerable glib talk today about the problems of the highly selective institution. Harvard University accepts one out of nine students who apply, and is in a position where it could, if it wished, accept only the upper 1 per cent of high school graduating classes. This is only a recent phenomenon, however; in the early 1950s Harvard was accepting one of three students who applied.

Or consider such developing state institutions as the New England state universities. Until the end of the 1950s, these institutions were primarily concerned with teacher preparation, agriculture, and engineering for undergraduates. Within a very few years these institutions find themselves struggling to accommodate enrollment increases of several thousand each year, induction of new faculty at the rate of two or three hundred each year, and change of character from relatively single-purpose institutions to full multiversity status.

To exert strong leadership for change in the process of education in the face of these other institutional changes probably requires the creation of new kinds of leaders. But as John Gardner pointed out in his concluding report as president of the Carnegie Corporation, society is not training leaders. It is clearly demonstrable that society is not training people to carry on some of the specialized functions in the increasingly complex institutions. The role of director of institutional research is a case in point. Institutional research is a new technique designed to improve college management, but colleges and universities simply have not trained technically competent people to do the tasks inherent in the concept of institutional research.

Even if leaders could generate change in teaching, little is known about how to do such things as provide adequate in-service training for faculties. A number of techniques have been attempted

—faculty seminars, libraries of pedagogical materials, faculty conferences, and the like—but there is little evidence that any of the techniques have validity.

Still another barrier is the breakdown of communication between people, particularly as institutions become more complex. Existing channels become clogged very quickly and there seems to be a reluctance on the part of people, particularly administrators, to make overt efforts to unclog channels of communication. Barriers resulting from bureaucratic structure are intensified by the differences in the several academic disciplines. There probably are on the college campus not just two cultures but several hundred, and these several hundred cultures find it difficult to communicate with each other.

Another barrier is the confusion regarding types of institutions. As one thinks about college education one is inclined to generalize about the enterprise as though all institutions were quite similar, and there is some reason to believe that institutions are becoming more like each other—that is, complex, multipurpose institutions. Technical institutes such as M.I.T., Carnegie Tech, and Cal Tech have become comprehensive universities by adding large increments of the humanities and social sciences. Former teachers' colleges have added liberal arts, business, and graduate work. Liberal arts colleges have added teacher education, business, and home economics—one college has even added agriculture. Even junior colleges seem to follow this pattern of regression toward the mean. But there are still fundamental differences.

Recall that there are approximately 2,200 institutions of higher education in this country, of which eight hundred are two-year institutions making no pretensions of having a research function. Then there are something on the order of 850 single-purpose, liberal arts colleges. With the exception of a very small number, perhaps thirty to fifty at the most, these institutions make no pretensions of forcing faculties to engage in research. Yet, in most of these institutions there is a tendency for people to excuse themselves from being creative teachers on the grounds that they need to pursue their own research. Paul Woodring demonstrated the ridiculousness of such an excuse by pointing out that if every faculty member in the country produced an article every year, the number of learned journals would have to be increased by ten thousand. If every faculty member produced a book every five years, the number of publishers would have to be doubled. This barrier is exemplified by the young assistant professor who remarked that he would just as soon not be regarded as a scintillating teacher; that would allow at least the presumption that he was a brilliant researcher.

The last barrier to innovation in teaching is the academic conscience. Regardless of the specific religious denominations to which American professors give allegiance, there is a strong vein of Calvinism in most of them. There is a feeling among professors that a certain number of hours must be put in on the job each week, hence the argument that the committee system is really a salve to the Calvinistic conscience of the college professor. He puts in his classroom time during the morning, which can be a drain if he has to talk to four or five hundred students. Ideally, in the afternoon he should spend his time thinking, reading, just loafing, or doing something else. But such activities, rejuvenating though they may be, are not really work in the Calvinistic sense, and so a committee is the ideal substitute. In a committee one does not have to think, but one is required to be present and to go through the motions of work.

These barriers to change—and the list could be elaborated—have become so obstinate that some institutions have begun to experiment by actually institutionalizing change agents. Some institutions are trying to create what one theorist called a "Vice-President for Heresy," and much of the effort of the United States Office of Education and foundations such as the Danforth Foundation are directed toward bringing about change in education.

There is increasing acceptance of the belief that education is an important tool of national policy which should be used to solve vexing domestic problems. Yet, there is the awareness that education as it has been practiced in the past is probably not effective. Even a gross organization for learning might work with a student population which comes for the most part from middle- and upper-class homes, because those students have had experience with books and other artifacts from infancy. But to solve the problems of educating the culturally disadvantaged, whether these disadvantaged be Negroes in large northern cities, poor whites from Appalachia, small farmers from the backwoods of Maine, Indians in New Mexico, or

Puerto Ricans in New York City, requires different and more refined techniques than education has thus far used.

The problem of change demands effort along several fronts. There must be basic research to find means of educating, but there must also be dissemination of information and techniques which are currently known, and experimentation with ways of gaining faculty acceptance of relevant new techniques. Without minimizing the values of research, we propose to deal in the following chapters with the development part of research and development—that is, what is now known and what can be done about it.

V

The Rigid Curriculum

The organization of the undergraduate curriculum and the rules governing it have grown up partially because of the professionalization of faculty and partially because of historical accident. Studies about college students and their criticisms of curriculum show that reforms are imperative; the contrast between professorial ideals and student versions of Utopia is marked.

The largest number of books about higher education are written by academicians who describe educational ideals in theoretical and philosophic terms. Most of them hold traditional academic viewpoints sharply opposed to student demands for freer, varied, realistic educational experiences. Elton Trueblood argues for a faculty-imposed curriculum on the grounds that most eighteen-year-olds arriving at college are neither sufficiently educated nor experienced to choose a curriculum. He recommends a "combination of limited electives and increasing concentration in one field" near the end of college as "a more ideal curriculum." He also advocates, with "good psychological reason," that technical subjects should come first and "humanizing studies" later.[1]

A voice more alien to those seeking change is that of Leo Strauss.[2] Strauss describes liberal education as "the necessary endeavor to found an aristocracy within democratic mass society," and says it aims at producing "a cultured human being" who has studied "the great books which the greatest minds have left behind." Such education, he writes, "will always remain the obligation and privilege of a minority" which will remind "those members of a mass democracy who have ears to hear of human greatness." It is, he said, the "counter-poison to mass culture."

Russell Kirk, in *The Intemperate Professor*, declares that "the college should return to a curriculum emphasizing classical literature, languages, moral philosophy, history, the pure sciences, logic, rhetoric, and religious knowledge." Colleges should reject "survey courses, general education, and similar substitutes for real intellectual discipline" because this "smattering . . . produces the little learning which is a dangerous thing." Kirk defines the aim of liberal education as "ethical consciousness through which the student is brought to . . . enduring truths which govern our being [and] the principles of self-control and the dignity of man." He also asserts the value of knowledge—even "useless knowledge"—for its own sake. He calls the college away from vocationalism which he says belongs to trade schools and industrial training and from "specialized and professional studies which are the proper province of the graduate schools of universities."

Kirk also rejects "quasi-commercial programs of athletics" as antiintellectual, expensive, and in vain competition with "behe-

[1] E. Trueblood, *The Idea of a College* (New York: Harper and Row, 1956).

[2] L. Strauss, "Liberal Education and Mass Democracy," in R. A. Goldwin (Ed.), *Higher Education and Modern Democracy* (Chicago: Rand McNally, 1967).

moth" universities. He would reject students who cannot get into a great university or state college and set college standards higher than those institutions. He would "deliberately" limit enrollment. And he would "reduce to a minimum" elective courses in obeisance to "order and hierarchy" and direct the young student who is incapable "of judging with discretion what his course of study ought to be." These curricula and strictures, devoted to "furnishing society with a body of tolerably well educated persons . . . to provide right reason and conscience in the Commonwealth," will, through their educated graduates, "remind the rising generation . . . of a great continuity . . . and that we moderates are only dwarfs mounted upon the shoulders of giants" of the past, says Kirk.[3]

A similar discrepancy can be found in the stated objectives of most undergraduate institutions and the procedures by which those objectives are achieved. It is likely that the language of some statements of objectives conforms to some of the expressed desires of undergraduate students, but this affinity is quickly dissipated on turning catalog pages to see how the program is implemented. Consider this statement, which is reasonably characteristic of the genre:

Blank University is a community of professing Christian scholars dedicated to a philosophy of liberal education. The major goals of the institution are to inculcate a respect for learning and truth; to free the mind from the confinements of ignorance and prejudice; to organize the powers of clear thought and expression; to preserve and extend knowledge; to help man achieve professional competence and to establish life-long habits of study, learning, and reflection. An emphasis on the liberating arts . . . seeks to develop creative, reflective, and responsible persons. At the same time, the acquisition of specialized . . . skills is recognized as a condition of successful involvement in the modern world. The university . . . encourages the pursuit of rich and ennobling experiences and the development of significant personhood through an appreciation of man's intellectual, artistic, cultural and natural surroundings. The university affirms its fundamental obligation to confront liberally educated

---

[3] R. Kirk, *The Intemperate Professor and Other Cultural Splenetics* (Baton Rouge: Louisiania State University Press, 1965).

*men with the challenges of Christian faith and to instill in them a
true sense of vocation.*

Then contrast that language with the language which really
counts:

*General university requirements: A candidate for a bachelor's de-
gree must present credit in approved courses amounting to a minimum of 128 semester hours, and have maintained a grade point
average of 2.00. He must meet the general requirements of one
year in residence, earning a minimum of 30 semester hours of credit
at the university during his senior year. A minimum of 40 semester
hours of upper division courses is required. Other general policies
regarding the eligibility for a bachelor's degree are: (1) No more
than 24 hours of correspondence and/or extension work may be
counted for a bachelor's degree. (2) Nonmusic majors are limited to
8 hours credit toward graduation for participation in music en-
sembles.*

This is followed by department requirements and the omnipresent
list of courses offered.

Although printed statements of purposes of colleges and
universities in catalogs exert no great force either in directing what
the college does or in helping students understand what the college
is, the very phrasing of typical statements reveals a limited and
distorted view of human development. One church-related college
talks about preparing students for service and leadership in professions; qualifying them to enter graduate schools; improving
fundamental skills and capacity to transmit understanding; aiding in
the development of appreciation of scientific methods; developing
qualities of citizenship; and cultivating a sensitivity to spiritual
values.

A private comprehensive university, after a prologue which
speaks of developing each individual's unique capacities, then speci-
fies more precisely the traits the institution seeks to develop. These
are the ability to perceive alertly with inquiring minds which operate
through exact and accurate knowledge, thus allowing for reasoning
and wise evaluation. The institution wants students to learn to

articulate their ideas and feelings clearly and gracefully in writing and speaking. Ultimately, it wants students to place knowledge at the disposal of action. A small church-related college for women holds as its fundamental purpose the development of self-educating Christian persons who are dedicated to the discovery of truth and the service of others. A comprehensive public university emphasizes early entry into advanced academic work, superior preparation for graduate or professional training, clear and correct prose, precise thinking, interdependence and integration of all knowledge, development of responsible citizenship, and the exciting challenge of intellectual discovery.

These things which colleges claim they are trying to do are not bad things; no one can really quarrel with rationality, intellectuality, knowledge, or good citizenship. One cannot really be against developing scholarly competence. But a number of words which do seem appropriate in the light of student testimony are noticeable by their absence—beauty, feeling, friendship, play, pleasure, enjoyment, appreciation, and affection seldom appear. Yet it is this sort of word which names the experience that many late-adolescent youth are asking for and hope the college will help them find. Student testimony on the values of friendship is so eloquent as to need no further remark. Students are demanding help to feel deeply and fully, to help clarify their own identities so that they can enjoy and take pleasure from the world in which they find themselves.

It can be argued that the college is, after all, an institution of limited mission, and that it can only concern itself with knowledge and rationality. If so, then colleges should reject what so many of them claim—that they are interested in the development of the whole man. The only judgment that one can really make about colleges and universities on the basis of their stated purposes and goals is that American colleges and universities are awfully academic, rational, and dull. Maybe this is what they are, but the question is, Should they be? If they should be joyful, should not statements of objectives indicate this?

Then there is the matter of the order of courses. Because of college preoccupation with rationality and because of the belief that fundamental learning must be acquired first, there is a strong tendency to place single-discipline or fundamentals courses early in the curriculum on the assumption that a student's subsequent work should build on these. Thus, in a nondifferentiated liberal arts program, a freshman student would be expected to take rhetoric, organic chemistry, a foreign language, mathematics, and history of civilization. But are these courses really the most appropriate means of helping freshmen to develop? It now seems that courses having a heavier load of emotion would be more in harmony with the developmental needs of college-age youth. During the freshman year, courses in art, music, or philosophy, if geared to exploring the questions of young people, might be appropriate. There probably is ample time later in the college career for the young person to develop the necessary cognitive skills which seemingly come from single-discipline courses.

There are serious obstacles to such a reversal of practice. Students in engineering, several of the hard sciences, and teacher preparation typically have such prescribed and theoretically sequential programs that they must begin intensive work in the discipline as freshmen. But while this necessity is compelling, it is not as compelling as faculties allow themselves to believe. A student planning to major in chemistry could take a year's course in mathematics, a year's sequence in physics and chemistry, and even a year's sequence in rhetoric, and still be allowed two-fifths of his entire program for the feeling-laden courses. And there is no discernible, demonstrable reason why some contextual courses could not be taken with courses in the major (modern algebra and modern physics could be taken at the same time). This is true in most of the verbally-oriented courses, for few of these fall into a sequential relationship. There is no reason why students could not take advanced psychology courses with statistics and research design, or why they could not have history, economics, and political science at the same time and toward the last part of the undergraduate career.

Students are also asking for greater leisure to move at their own pace and to still have time for deeper penetration into subjects which interest them. The typical pattern for an undergraduate college on a semester system is for students to take five and even six courses at a time, each course meeting three or four hours a week.

The net result is that they are constantly on the move from one course to another and their out-of-class preparation is apt to be highly fragmented.

Although educational practices are culturally based and cannot be directly transplanted from one culture to another, it is possible to learn from the successes and failures of other educational efforts. An essential part of the Oxford or Cambridge style of education is sufficient leisure, so that students, under the guidance of tutors, can probe deeply into the subject they are studying. Students testify that they probably misuse leisure during the earlier part of their careers at these English institutions, but eventually they sense the possibilities of an uncluttered space of time and they begin to work. Colleges might well reduce the number of required courses, as some institutions have done, and then expect students to delve more deeply into the remaining subjects with greater learning and satisfaction.

Since the student peer group is such a potent force in student development, the curriculum should be reorganized to maximize the use of peer groups for educational purposes. Cluster colleges, house plans, and team teaching have demonstrated the feasibility of grouping as a technique of pedagogy. Florida State University is making use of the routine device of block scheduling the same students into the same courses to create an accidental friendship or primary group. The result is greater across-the-board achievement. Team teaching in the College of Basic Studies at Boston University has year after year brought dramatic gains on the part of students who were not eligible to enter a bachelor's degree program as freshmen. The close relationship between the eight faculty members and one hundred students who worked together for two years as a group, following a prescribed curriculum, generated a force which was reflected in higher academic achievement and in higher achievement on various sorts of tests. The house plan at Stephens College similarly brings one hundred students and five faculty members into the close relationship which creates residence hall esprit de corps and produces measurably greater achievement on common tasks than students in other parts of the institution demonstrate.

It is argued that the department system already provides this grouping of people with similar interests, but one must be skeptical of this claim. At large, complex institutions only the few students who join a department club see each other frequently. In the smaller institutions the number of department majors is likely to be so small as to prevent the formation of the requisite critical mass. It also might be argued that large institutions are so complex it is impossible to organize groups of students who can enjoy a sustained relationship. It is true that there are difficulties, but once a ratio of faculty to students is established, this ratio may be manipulated in different ways to accomplish some of this salutary grouping.

Formal face-to-face meetings of classes can be organized for greater impact. In the orthodox style, students attend class three, four, or five hours each week in a regular pattern for each of the five or six courses they take. This frequency of confrontation seems to insure that no class session is likely to be highly potent. This pattern virtually precludes the possibility for what Benjamin S. Bloom has called a "peak learning experience." Bloom observed that once in a while a learning situation has such impact that it commands the full mental and emotional attention of the individual, and that subsequent testing reveals students to have almost complete recall of what they had been working on. Students can not take too many of these experiences, however, for the experiences are generally accompanied by a reaction. If the number of face-to-face contacts in the formal classroom situation were limited, the instructor could prepare more thoroughly and the impact of the class session could be substantially heightened. For example, college courses might bring students and faculty face-to-face in the classroom no more than an hour and a half each week. Students could spend time out of class working on their own or under the personal guidance of the professor.

Such an idea is threatening to both students and faculty. It means that under the existing schemes students would spend about seven hours in class each week, which raises the spectre of students misusing their time and drifting into useless behavior. The open schedule also threatens faculty members who find that routinely meeting their classes is easier than long preparation for a single appearance.

A related matter is length of courses. A prevalent tendency is to offer one-semester or one-quarter courses, which contributes to the fragmentation of a student's education. In a typical semester arrangement, students take five or six courses each semester, several of which are one-semester courses, or the student chooses one semester of a two-semester sequence. So, in a nine-month period a student is expected to become proficient in seven or eight different subjects. Consider the reality of a one-semester course in, say, economics of labor. Ideally (and the ideal is rarely achieved), a student spends approximately 135 hours in study and in class in the expectation that he will master at least some basic principles. More likely the student spends 90 or fewer hours during a full semester in study and in class. Of course, there is a need for some semester or quarter-length courses, but in order to provide time for the necessary immersion in a subject, the majority of undergraduate courses should be year-long sequences. With year-long sequences and no more than three courses at a time, the student would have the desired and needed leisure for deeper inquiry.

In some respects, mathematics, the hard sciences, and foreign languages have dictated part of the structure of the undergraduate curriculum. Because mathematics is a sequential subject, with the clear necessity for one course to build on another, and because advanced work in chemistry, physics, and to some degree biology requires prior experience, the prerequiste system has been applied indiscriminately throughout the undergraduate curriculum, thereby imposing this rigidity on subjects which do not need it. This is not to say that valid argument does not support sequential courses and prerequisites, but as a general rule, the practice should be questioned. For example, there appears to be no justification for requiring a course on major British authors as a prerequisite to a course devoted to a critical reading of the comedies and histories of William Shakespeare. Nor does one laboratory science course seem truly necessary as a prerequisite for a course on the history of science. Very likely a large proportion of verbally-oriented courses could be listed without prerequisites, thus opening opportunities for imaginative program planning.

The often arbitrary division of courses into upper division and lower division, with accompanying regulations, also might be examined. Such a practice neglects the developmental purposes of education. A so-called upper-division course conceivably might be appropriate for some freshmen or sophomore students, and even a graduate student close to the doctorate could use and enjoy a sophmore course on medieval history, if that particular experience were what he needed. Eliminating the division of courses by levels could help free the curriculum from unnecessary regulation and make it easier to plan programs in the interest of the student.

Of a somewhat different order is the matter of discontinuities in the undergraduate experience.

In the traditional academic program, students move steadily from the freshman through the senior year in a four-year sequence at the same college. (Professors really are not happy if some of their students receive educational experiences at another institution.) But in reality students have made interrupted education the rule rather than the exception. Less than 50 per cent of today's college freshmen will receive the bachelor's degree four years from now. However, in some institutions 65 or 70 per cent of these freshmen will receive the bachelor's degree within the next ten years. The rapidly growing public junior colleges are one institutionalized way of allowing for discontinuity. Gradually, institutions are creating other means of discontinuity, such as study abroad, a cooperative work-study experience, a mandatory leave of absence, or a leave of absence to allow for such things as Peace Corps service. The essential aim of fruitful interruptions is the opportunity for a complete change of pace from steady course work in order to help students assimilate the developmental steps taken in their formal courses.

Allowing for unusual exceptions, we can urge that each institution specifically provide for every student to have at least one radically different off-campus experience during his bachelor's degree program. This experience can be a semester abroad; a semester at a different location while doing cadet teaching; a semester or year of planned work experience; or an interim period used for such things as mapping an unexplored territory or serving as a participant-observer in the poor people's march on Washington. As institutions plan discontinuities, however, they should resist the temptation to convert interim period activities into variants of the course arrangement. Several institutions, for example, moved within

three years from a flexible interim period to the point where a catalog of courses was published for the interim period. Such a development simply perpetuates the worst features of the course system.

Two other matters deserve brief comment, even though they
are quite obvious. Institutions do attract different sorts of students,
yet there is a strong tendency for colleges to pattern their curricula
after the prestigious or visible institutions, whether or not those
patterns are appropriate. It is likely that accrediting associations
have contributed to this practice. A small institution serving youth
from a rural area, for instance, can serve students better than by requiring two years of a foreign language for graduation simply because other types of colleges do so.

The emergence of black power in the United States has
given voice to a different kind of curriculum criticism. The militant
black student says that the curriculum is designed with the needs of
white middle-class Americans in mind, and it relies exclusively on
materials dealing with the white Western tradition. He calls for
courses which stress African traditions, Negro history, Negro contributions to society, and Negro artistic expressions and modes of
thought. Now, if these militant Negroes are even partially correct,
and there is reason to suspect they are, we should look at the undergraduate curriculum with a view to stressing materials relevant to
the subcultures from which substantial numbers of students come.
Institutions might give greater attention to understanding the background characteristics of their student body and making accom-
modations in the curriculum for them. A small Minnesota liberal
arts college which attracts 80 per cent of its students from Swedish-
American farm families, for instance, might well base some of its
course work on the values of that subculture. Similarly, certain New
York City institutions might stress Jewish, Puerto Rican, or Irish
cultures and traditions.

Students, particularly radical students, charge that an unfortunate homogenization of American life is taking place, and that
it is apparent in the marked similarity of college catalogs. If this
trend is unfortunate, then it might be modified if institutions would
attempt to reflect in curricula the subcultures relevant to them. We
can hope that the institution outside Detroit stressing cultural values
from Central Europe, the southern California institution stressing

Mexican-American values, and the urban institution in San Francisco stressing Oriental and Afro-American values can each achieve excellence in different ways. The need of all students for a common universe of discourse can be provided through general education requirements, and the unique needs of students from various subcultures can be met in other portions of the curriculum.

Human needs are remarkably consistent; nevertheless, some needs and desires do shift over the generations and such changes should be accommodated in the college curriculum. In the past there has been a remarkable cultural lag in colleges and universities, exemplified by the requirement—lasting into the 1920s in some institutions—that applicants have a working knowledge of both Latin and Greek. This is not to disparage classical learning and languages but to suggest that the classics no longer have the utility for life in the United States that they did for life in the American colonies. The demand on the part of the students for changing content of courses to coincide with changing conditions and needs is well illustrated by the free university type of course, a course outside the academic structure, designed to provide material that students view as relevant. Some courses of this type may strike academicians as bizarre and not really "education."

Consider, for example, several recent course descriptions from the Mid-Peninsular Free University in California:

The Naked Ape *is a provocative current work by the British sociologist Desmond Morris. His basic thesis is that unless we understand our biological basis, we cannot hope to cope with our current social and political problems. In this group we will consider what man is biologically, and therefore what choices he has. This is a continuing class from last quarter and enrollment is closed. Meets Sunday at 7:30.*

A political science course is labeled "Have You Seen Behind the Hilton, Mr. Brown?" and the course description is:

The seminar will investigate the problems of the powerless and create a program to educate the middle-class community, confronting them with their complicity in sustaining those problems. The course includes the following: (1) a weekend in core poverty areas of San Francisco, (2) solid research into specific problem areas selected by the group, (3) discussion of issues with deep probing of individual attitudes and awarenesses, (4) formulation of a specific educational presentation, perhaps including film, slides, and interviews to be used.

And a philosophy and psychology course is entitled "Humanity and Rationality." Its course description reads:

Is it possible to have a religion that can be established by scientific standards? Are all opinions necessarily only emotionally based? Truly, the straight rational person is screwing himself by being straight. Some of us know that we haven't begun to relate to each other. Unless we want to blow ourselves up or eat each other, it is imperative that we, especially the intellectual community which has the talents and knowledge to help in the process, recognize and accept the truth, viz., I live, (not I think, therefore I am) and the corollary imperative of cultural deconditioning by whatever means necessary.

Similar courses are being offered or have been recommended at highly respected institutions and seem to have gained some student support. Antioch College reorganized its entire freshman year and developed courses which depart from orthodox norms and attempt to speak to changed conditions. For the spring of 1969, for example, such courses as these were offered: "Reading Poetry Aloud," "Pop Music—Pop Culture," "Alienation and Self-Alienation; the Jewish Experience," "Collisions on a Pool Table," "Electoral Politics," "Who Rules?" and "Black Ghetto."

The course "Electoral Politics" is described this way:

Content: research, participation in and analysis of the national political campaign and of the Cecile for Congress campaign here in the Seventh District. Analysis of voting patterns. The course will also include a postelection analysis of what happened and why. Process: the course will involve lectures and discussions every week as well as sessions in which actual experiences in the campaign will be discussed and analyzed. Discussions will be led by student initiators and associated faculty. Dan Grady will present research data on the Seventh District.

The University of California, Berkeley, not especially noted for its educational experimentation, recommended through its select committee the immediate creation of ad hoc courses dealing with matters which had aroused the interest of significant elements of the student body. It was suggested that course titles might be "The Idea and Uses of the University," "Vietnam," "Literary Censorship," "The City," and "Sino-Soviet-American Relations." [4]

Conditions do change and subject matter that makes up the curriculum can and should be changed to meet those conditions. This may involve a radical departure from traditional ways of dividing human knowledge into manageable units, but there is no convincing evidence that those orthodox ways are the best. Of course, it can be said that there is no convincing evidence for new divisions. Nonetheless, experimentation with such new types of offerings seems mandated if student concerns are to be taken seriously.

The Antioch freshman year program also includes a structural device which might have relevance for other institutions. The premise is that different courses require different lengths of time, from one or two weeks to one or two years. We can conceive of an undergraduate curriculum in which students might take several courses throughout an academic year, and also take ten or fifteen other curricular experiences of shorter duration. Such a concept will, of course, bother those concerned with scheduling and the like. But it is possible, especially with the aid of computers, to provide flexible scheduling to accommodate these different-length courses. Dwight Allen remarks:

A number of alternatives were made routinely possible only through the use of computer scheduling: for example, large and small classes, long and short classes, modular curriculum units, new combinations of staff, more intense use of facilities, the addition of independent study periods, nonstandard courses (longer or shorter than a standard semester, with more or less than the now-standard five hours a week of instruction), a wider variation in the number of classes each student can take, and so forth. [5]

[4] Select Committee.
[5] D. W. Allen, "Computer-Built Schedules and Educational Innovations," in D. D. Bushnell and D. W. Allen (Eds.), *The Computer in American Education* (New York: Wiley, 1967), p. 54.

He then proceeds to demonstrate how the computer was used to provide flexible scheduling and a high degree of individualization of instruction.

Then there is the rarely used device of scheduling optional sequences of lectures. Once again the English experience is instructive. The university schedules year-long series of lectures in subjects deemed of general interest. Students are expected to attend them only if they and their tutors believe it is desirable. Scheduling a series of lectures in such common subjects as American history and allowing students the option of attending if they feel a lack in their own intellectual development would be an appropriate substitute for placing American history among the required general education courses.

To emphasize an earlier point, it appears that much greater use of affective courses is appropriate for the undergraduate curriculum, especially during the early years of a student's career. Greater use of literature in the freshman and sophomore years seems wise, if these courses lead students to read a wide range of materials and to find idioms which speak to them. Greater opportunity to participate in studio experiences in the arts can also serve as a healthy counterpoint to exclusive and arid rationality. Rather than presenting a list of curriculum possibilities which could emphasize emotion, we mention just one—jazz, the only indigenous American musical form, a highly spontaneous form of music which speaks to the feelings of its performers and hearers. Yet few colleges or universities offer courses in jazz, feeling that it somehow lacks respectability. Ralph Gleason says:

It is challenging to contemplate what might be the result of some active, planned effort to encourage, rather than to discourage, the musically creative youth in our society. It is of interest to speculate what might be the result if "jazz education" were brought within the walls of our better high schools and colleges. It may be explosive to reconsider and to design appropriately educational experiences for truly creative youth in any form of art or in any educational discipline.[6]

[6] Heist, p. 98.

VI

Prevailing
Curriculum
Analysis

Thus far we have indicated some of the issues, practices, and current models that are operative within the wide framework of college and university curriculum and have provided a profile, based both on observation and on clinical data, of the search for self which seems so typical of the developmental needs of the college student of the 1970s. We now examine in some detail the prevailing approaches to an analysis of the curriculum.

The establishment, operation, and evaluation of the curriculum ought to be central responsibilities of college faculties and academic administration since the curriculum is the vehicle through which the institution seeks to make its most significant impact on the lives of students. Yet student testimony, as we have indicated previously, does not assign a high value to the curriculum as such. In institutions as varied as Stanford, Antioch, Michigan State, Harvard, and Cornell other factors are judged of greater worth. Nor are faculties and administrative officers at all sure how to make up a curriculum and how to analyze and change it. In many respects, curricula, especially for undergraduates, just grow in response to the organic needs or desires or interests of the individual members of the faculty as it is constituted at any one time. As generations of faculty move on, their memories are perpetuated by the continued catalog listing of courses which reflected their individual tastes and styles. Perhaps there can be no curriculum other than one which reflects faculty interest and talent. But such a premise runs strongly counter to an equally strong conviction that education is, or should be, a rational process. And it is disputed by the serious efforts of administrators to modify the curriculum.

Perhaps the most widely used technique of curriculum study, other than the administrative review process by which new courses each year are added to the aggregate, is a self-study. Whether it be mounted in response to the requirements of an accrediting association, to the offer of philanthropic dollars, or to an internal feeling of a need for change, the self-study provides an opportunity to talk about the curriculum. The general pattern is to divide a portion of the faculty into a number of committees, of which the curriculum committee is one and the committee on objectives or purposes or goals is another. Those committees meet, talk, and circulate reports which eventually are bound and become the self-study report. The committee on purposes is supposed to establish the philosophical charter which governs what the curriculum committee decides should be the curriculum content. Since committees are talking simultaneously about all parts of the college, it sometimes happens that radical change does suggest itself. But frequently, since a curriculum involves vested interests of quite personal significance to power blocs within the institution, the self-study becomes political action of a conservative sort.

A modification of the full self-study technique is the use of a few temporary committees charged specifically with preparing recommendations on the curriculum for later consideration by the full faculty. Many institutions have undertaken this type of study with the aid of an outside consultant. Members of each committee prepare position papers which are then debated and finally reconciled by a steering committee. Through this process broad policy statements which the college can endorse gradually emerge. In a study at Knox College, the first decision was to accept an increase in institutional size as a necessary prologue to curriculum reform.

A less often utilized approach but one which is appealing in its directness and simplicity is the use of an outside consultant. In one institution, the president was able to develop the physical plant and the financial structure, but he was unable to stimulate the faculty to look at the curriculum. He invited in a consultant who spent much time with departments and divisions and then suggested the composition of the curriculum and the ways by which the faculty might prepare itself to offer the curriculum. Another institution secured a small foundation grant to support a panel of consultants with the stipulation that the college would implement whatever curriculum recommendations the consultants suggested. Here, of course, the validity of the study rests on the wisdom of the consultant, and the effectiveness of any change rests on the amount of faculty respect he can command.

In another college which also experienced faculty reluctance to ponder the curriculum, the board of trustees organized itself into working committees and attempted to recommend curriculum structure. Using staff support from a director of institutional research and the critical insights of a panel of consultants, the board committee attempted to establish policy guidelines for the curriculum on the assumption that the faculty would later implement them. This scheme possesses the obvious advantage of using appropriate power but the clear danger that a faculty will be suspicious of whatever a board suggests. Further, a board committee, regardless of the dedication of its members, simply cannot spend the enormous amount of time which conversation about a curriculum entails.

One college elected a unique form of curriculum analysis which made a different use of a panel of experts. A staff officer prepared a profile of the college and its supporting community. This profile was submitted to a panel of professors from other colleges with the request that they recommend what courses and programs should be offered. The reasoning was that the experts, not affected by local community pressures, would be able to make an objective appraisal.

Using a different panel, W. W. Charters attempted to base the curriculum of Stephens College on the needs of college educated women. He asked several hundred women to keep diaries of their activities. Then, he classified and codified these records into nine clusters of activities which became the structure for the curriculum. The courses developed were intended to speak to the behaviors of women.

Similarly, looking to the needs of the people, the role and scope study of the Florida higher education system sought, through economic and social analysis, to identify the kinds of vocations Florida needed. This division was then used to indicate the broad division of curriculum responsibility for each public institution. Many locally controlled junior colleges have developed their criteria in the same way. Courses and programs are offered in accordance with the requests and needs of the supporting community. The trick is to determine what a community does want, for any aggressive faculty member can generate some expression of interest in almost any subject. Further, the difference between a verbal expression of interest and utilization of programs is often great. Thus, extension services in engineering science might be demanded by a local industry but not used by the people they were intended to help.

A sophisticated approach to curriculum study is represented by a Columbia University study of general education. A faculty committee was appointed and a distinguished sociologist was granted released time to provide the staff work. He looked at general education as it was offered in several similar institutions, the problems which his own college had faced in the past, and the changed conditions of higher education throughout the nation. In the light of all this, the committee made a series of recommendations which then became the subject of faculty debate. Generally such monumental studies have provided more guidance for other institutions than for the campus which sponsored the study. For example, the Harvard report, *General Education in a Free Society,* made the concept of general education respectable but did not substantially affect the Harvard curriculum.

The history of the Harvard report underscores the most widely used device for curriculum construction: what is being done elsewhere. A dean of a new college first collects catalogs of colleges which he regards as similar to his own and then constructs his curriculum based on normative averages. Or, a new course or program is described at a conference or in a journal article and immediately adopted by other similar (and dissimilar) institutions. Courses and programs on data-processing in junior colleges and honors programs in liberal arts colleges seem to have evolved in this way. Although the United States does not maintain a ministry of education, curriculum practice is remarkably uniform, largely, we suspect, because of the propensity of colleges to imitate each other. David Riesman likens the collegiate enterprise to a snake with each portion of its body seeking to catch up with the portion in front. Snakelike movement frequently means that the head, middle, and tail are at approximately the same place at the same time. Riesman's worry is that the head usually does not know where it is going.

Contemporary practice thus suggests that discussion, political action, judgment of experts, emulation, and search for social needs are the prevailing methods of curriculum analysis and development. There are, of course, refinements. St. Andrews College uses a panel of experts to talk with faculty about new courses. Faculty committees are taken to remote places to discuss their curriculum problems. The Danforth workshop on liberal education is an effective agency in this regard. Teams from twenty-five colleges are brought to Colorado Springs each summer for three weeks of intensive shoptalk. Such a workshop does, however, foster further normative curriculum-building since what is done at one place seems attractive to professors at other institutions.

Several significant attempts have been made to develop a theory of curriculum, although generally these have not been used as a basis for curriculum analysis. Perhaps the most widely quoted are the insights of Alfred North Whitehead, who emphasizes the rhythm of education and its cyclic quality. He sees the states of romance, precision, and generalization following one another throughout life and setting the form and substance of each level of education. Thus, the infant first enjoys the romance of new objects for himself, then moves to precision as he perceives objects, and then to the form of generalization in the form of language as it seeks to classify objects. For those who continue beyond secondary school, the college or university course represents a period of generalization, and a spirit of generalization should dominate the university. Courses should assume a familiarity with details and should not bore students by forcing them to go over specifics they have already studied. The function of the university is to allow one to shed details in favor of principles. But he is not suggesting a prescribed curriculum for everyone. Whitehead sees at least three curricula—literary, scientific, and technical—and by implication subdivisions of these. At the college level, each should address the generalizing function. Throughout the *Aims of Education* Whitehead suggests approaches and even modes of teaching various subjects. Thus, if one teaches Latin, he justifies the reading of much Latin literature in translation, but at no time does he present justification for including one course over another.

John Henry Cardinal Newman also has things to say about the curriculum. But, aside from arguing that theology has a key place in the curriculum, that a university should contain all branches of knowledge, and that students should not take too many subjects, his theories are of scant help to one who would build a curriculum. Indeed, at one point he suggests that if he had a choice between a university which stressed a wide range of subjects for all students and one which did absolutely nothing save tolerate students to live together, he would opt for the latter. He does believe, as does Whitehead, that a college subject should emphasize generalization or, in his terms, philosophy, and that one subject should relate to all others. He further sees a three-way division of subjects into God (theology), nature (science), and man (the humanities or literature). As to which subjects within science and the humanities students should study, his theories provide no help. His lectures are more a guide to the structure of a university and a guide to teaching than a guide to the precise formulation of a curriculum.

A more recent formulation is that by Ralph W. Tyler, who argues that the objectives of education are value choices beyond which one cannot go. They are conditioned by such factors as the needs of society, the needs of individuals, and the laws of learning. If a college develops a set of objectives which differ radically from those of another institution, there is really no way of validating one set against the other. Once objectives are stated, however, there is a clear way of converting them into curriculum form. First, they must be specified into descriptions of behavior, then realistic learning experiences which will produce the desired behavior must be identified, and finally, these experiences must be consolidated into patterns or courses. To Tyler, there are appropriate and inappropriate ways of achieving objectives, and the most effective curriculum is the one which best achieves whatever objectives are set for it. By implication, Tyler would argue that the first and most difficult step in establishing a curriculum is deciding what goals should be sought. After agreement on this score, curriculum construction is an engineering problem.

Several contemporary theorists address themselves to perfecting the engineering of the curriculum. Paul L. Dressel, who directly continues Tyler's emphasis on behavioral objectives and outcomes, sees ten problems which must be solved if a curriculum is to be viable: the gap between liberal and vocational education must be bridged; course and credit hour structure must be loosened; common experiences must be provided; continuity, sequence, and integrity should be ensured; fewer blocs of subjects should be the rule; courses should be more infused with psychologically sound learning devices; values should be considered; preoccupation with the West should be combined with non-Western emphases; better learning facilities should be created; costs should be considered. As a tool to solve these problems, he uses a set of conservative limiting principles, such as a fixed proportion of work to be taken in common by all students to establish curriculum limits. Then, within those limits, he would have the faculty, following a Tyler sort of analysis, decide what the content of courses should be.

Earl McGrath ends up with a similar set of limiting principles through a somewhat different mode of analysis. McGrath, looking at desirable, commonly accepted outcomes of undergraduate education, finds that achievement of those outcomes bears little relationship to the number of specific courses a department offers, although the number of courses is related to the cost of education. Hence, for economic reasons, he arrives at a concept of a limited curriculum, the content of which can be changed as conditions change, but the size of which must remain constant.

There are other less engineering-styled theories of curriculum. Robert J. Henle identifies five different approaches to reality, each of which must be given statement in the curriculum. The humanistic approach deals with concrete reality. The philosophical approach is an activity of pure reflective intelligence working upon experience. Science is also a discipline of pure intelligence, but it acts upon interrelationships of facts. Theology deals not with experience but with data accepted from God. Mathematics is also a discipline of pure intelligence which develops a purely intellectual world of intelligible entities applicable to the physical world. To order these approaches into a curriculum requires a theory of knowledge based upon personal experience with ways of knowing. To select from among the five approaches and to balance the effort, Henle suggests several principles: subjects should reveal the ultimate meaning and explanation of human life and reality; courses should provide students with personal experience appropriate to each approach to reality; courses should relate the student to his own environment and prepare him to live in his own culture; courses should be chosen for inclusion in the curriculum because of the magnitude of their possible impact on students and because of the likelihood that they will produce personal insights at basic points.[1]

Henle, with his Roman Catholic orientation, has a secular counterpart in Philip H. Phenix. For Phenix, the basis of human nature is that human beings discover, create, and express meanings. And meanings possess various dimensions. The first dimension is that of experience, which refers to the inner life, the life of the mind. Then there is rule, logic, or principle, which allows for categories of things. A third dimension is selective elaboration, which allows an unlimited combination of meanings. And the last dimension is expression, or communication.

Meanings also can be divided into realms which, in turn, become the structure of the formal curriculum. The first realm is symbolics, which comprises language and mathematics. The second, empirics, includes natural science. Then esthetics contains the arts; synoetics embraces personal knowledge; ethics includes moral mean-

[1] R. J. Henle, "Objectives of the Catholic Liberal Arts," in J. B. McGannon (Ed.), *Christian Wisdom and Christian Information* (New York: Sheed and Ward, 1964).

ings; and synoptics, the sixth realm, involves meanings which are comprehensively integrative. Since the available knowledge is so great in each of these realms of meaning, the prime task of the curriculum builder is to select from this richness that which should constitute the curriculum content. Phenix suggests that all content should be drawn from recognized disciplines, exemplify representative ideas of disciplines, reflect and reveal characteristic methods of inquiry, and appeal to the imagination of the student.[2]

There are also other, more casual theories of curriculum-building. The first abdicates responsibility for the content of the undergraduate curriculum by tailoring courses to fit the requirements of the graduate school or, in the case of junior colleges, to fit the demands of four-year institutions. This method assumes that the end of education is professional competence and that the responsibility for preparing people for such roles rests with specialized schools and departments. The undergraduate years simply provide students with the skills and knowledge which make work easier at the next stage. Were this rationale not so widely accepted, it would almost be a caricature to mention it seriously. Nonetheless, hundreds of liberal arts colleges are tempting financial ruin by following such a theory.

A second such theory is a thoughtful approach based upon Deweyan pragmatism, which holds that there is no finite body of information. Rather, knowledge emerges and evolves as individuals seek to accommodate their conception of reality. Therefore, there should be no formal curriculum but simply students and faculty in close proximity. As students discover what they wish to study they find an appropriate teacher and chart a course of action. In the past the curricula of Bennington and Sarah Lawrence were based upon this conception. It was also reflected by James Madison Woods, who argued that Stephens College had no curriculum but rather two thousand curricula—one for each young woman enrolled in the school. The most eloquent contemporary spokesman for this approach is Harold Taylor, and its most viable manifestation is the free university.

[2] P. H. Phenix, *Realms of Meaning* (New York: McGraw-Hill, 1964).

Any systematic theory of curriculum probably results in a better educational program than would growth without theory. The very act of thinking through the content of education in terms of a set of presuppositions and premises forces conscious choice. Whether one translates abstract principles into behavior or selects from specified bodies of knowledge or even tries to intuit what students want when they express a desire for any given experience, the result is probably clearer, more effective education. Hence, in one respect one could argue that once a theory has been adopted, whether by chance or temperament, the biggest curriculum problem has been solved.

This argument overlooks the fact, however, that putting a curriculum into effect requires the solution of still other theoretical problems and also of some quite serious practical ones. Among these is the problem of criteria. How does a liberal arts college with limited resources decide which subjects should be taught from among the enormous variety that could be? Basing curricula upon the demands of a graduate school, the interests of individual faculty, the drawing power of courses, or the existence of attractive text material seems to be a denial that a curriculum can possess an internal logic and consistency. Although each of these elements must be considered realistically, they are nonrational criteria for curriculum-building.

Allied with the problem of criteria is the matter of setting limits on a curriculum in the face of the increase in knowledge. How does one decide what to drop when, for example, an infusion of non-Western material must be added to the curriculum? Or, how close to the frontiers of an expanding subject should undergraduate courses be kept? The significance of this problem can be judged from the fact that some people are arguing that physics is moving so rapidly as a field that no college that is not a part of a graduate school should even attempt to teach it. The professors outside universities just are not and cannot be sufficiently abreast of new developments.

Then there is the political problem. Given the premises of academic freedom, professorial privilege, the pedagogical importance of a professor's enthusiasm for his subject, and department power over course offerings, how does a theoretical curriculum become a reality? In a few institutions some effort was made to develop a theoretical curriculum before the faculty was appointed. But as quickly as the first professors arrived, the theoretical idea was modified. Similarly, a group of division chairmen, working together for a summer in isolation from the campus, can create a structure, but once the faculty starts to discuss it, such matters as the possible displacement of individual faculty members, fears about budget problems, and even alumni pressures become operative.

Related to the political problem is that of administration. The two sources of official academic power are the central administration and the faculty. Although the central administration is in a position to visualize the total curriculum, the faculty is generally given responsibility for curriculum decisions. Thus, a central administration can know that an unbalanced curriculum is a serious financial drain on the entire institution; the trick is to manipulate the faculty into taking some action on the basis of this knowledge. The arrangement of a system which utilizes department thinking, a collegewide committee structure, and the knowledge of administrators is a problem for which no ideal solution has yet been found.

While these and kindred problems cannot be solved in the absolute, a start can be made, as starts have been made for other equally difficult and complicated human activities, by accumulating information. Just as the natural sciences rest on detailed observation of nature, so should an educational theory be derived from an observation of specifics. Until now, college faculties have not possessed much knowledge about the many factors which impinge on a curriculum. The idea of institutional research is not very old. Now, with a concept of institutional research, with improved techniques of social research, and with improved information systems, it seems possible to obtain a great deal of information as to how the curriculum is working. One must have faith, then, that a faculty faced with quantities of information will be able to make rational decisions about the curriculum it offers.

Consider how faculties may react if each year they are provided with evidence—routine cost accounting for each course, department, and division; brief, regularly written reports by lay advisory committees; yearly reports of alumni reactions to the various courses; periodic polls of student opinion taken throughout the year; yearly assessment of sophomores and seniors on standardized tests; and brief resumes of significant social and curriculum developments. Here is the stuff out of which eventual curriculum theory must be molded. Information of this sort can approximate for the general faculty the insights which previously have been the province of only the Whiteheads and Newmans.

VII

Innovation
Possibilities

If one had sampled college campuses in the 1930s, particularly the parts of the campus concerned with undergraduate education, one would have found a relatively limited and common pattern of practices. Students entered as freshmen and expected to finish the bachelor's degree at the end of four years. Each of the four academic years was divided into two semesters, although in perhaps a fourth of the nation's colleges and universities the nine-month academic year was divided into three quarters. Students normally took four or five courses each semester. These courses met in formal classrooms three or four hours a week, except for instruction in foreign languages, which normally met every day of the week, and instruction in laboratory science, which provided time for students to do experiments described in considerable detail in their laboratory notebooks.

The prevailing mode of instruction was a lecture or lecturette, regardless of whether the class was relatively large (two to four hundred students) or small (ten to fifteen students). In large universities big classes would be organized with one or two lectures a week, followed by discussion sections frequently led by young instructors without the Ph.D. or by a limited number of graduate assistants. Students were expected to study two hours every week for each hour of credit, but it was unusual if they did half that much work. Students were assessed by means of a midterm examination and a final examination, with an occasional book report or term paper required. The requirements for a bachelor's degree were a certain number of semester or quarter hours of credit and sometimes courses in each of two or three major domains of knowledge. Occasionally in some of the science courses, slides of natural phenomena were shown, and once in a great while a particularly relevant motion picture was displayed during class time. The blackboard was the most frequently used visual aid, but, again with the exception of mathematics, it was not typically used. When it was used, the instructor's hieroglyphics—which he called handwriting—made the resultant list of words, taxonomies, or diagrams all but completely unintelligible.

If one were to make a similar sampling in 1970 of college campuses across the United States, one would, with some interesting and notable exceptions, find that higher education is practiced in substantially the same way. A class in French begins with students singing a simple French song, followed by individual student translations of sentences from French to English and English to French, then a short period of dictation, ending with a few students reading in French from a French reader. A class in the history of civilization is organized with a major professor giving one or two lectures to a large group each week, followed by discussion sections (in many respects just smaller copies of the large lecture) led by junior faculty members or graduate assistants.

Students still spend additional time in laboratory science courses, but they continue to receive less credit for the time spent in the laboratory than for the time spent in the equal tranquility of the lecture hall. Smaller classes labeled *discussion* continue to exemplify a lecturette—a less well-organized lecture with one or two questions asked—better than they do a genuine group effort at solving problems. The academic year still begins in September and ends in late May or early June, and again, whether students actually do so or not, the vast majority intend at the time they begin their college work to finish the bachelor's degree in four years.

There is an added element, of course. Students in a number of institutions expect almost as a matter of manifest destiny that they will "go on to graduate school." Actually, however, a visitor from Mars who walked down the hallway of a classroom building at the University of Illinois in 1935 would have found instruction much as it is at Stanford University in 1970. The hallways of Morgan Park Junior College in the 1930s would have revealed substantially the same sounds and demonstrated the same student and teacher behavior which one can find in Foothill College in 1970.

Some claim that such commonalities are to be expected, and that they reveal, among other things, the universal and timeless character of education. After all, education in the 1930s dealt with people, as does education in the 1970s. Colleges and universities in the 1930s did produce men and women who manned the greatest army the world had ever seen, brought about revolutionary new practices in medicine, made America more productive than any other nation, and are maintaining a high level of affluence while at the same time trying to rectify social abuses. If that system of education worked is there any reason to change it?

Another point of view holds that even if it could be established that college teaching in the 1930s was perfectly appropriate for the objectives and missions of higher education, change is still required in practice because higher education in the 1970s is required to do so much more than in the past. Such an argument would list a number of new problems for which the older, comfortable style of teaching and learning may be inappropriate.

There is first of all the problem of attempting to provide some education for an entire population and to provide some post-high school education for a vast majority of the population, perhaps as much as 80 per cent of the college-age group. Within this group are those with such marginal cultural backgrounds that they are unfit to profit from such techniques as the formal lecture. Higher education in the 1930s did not need to concern itself with changing fundamental self-images of large numbers of clients. Yet education

today must help hundreds of thousands of minority students overcome an image of themselves as inferior and a breed apart from the
majority of the population.

Although conditions were beginning to change in the 1930s,
those who attended college generally expected to receive their
bachelor's degree in business, education, or agriculture, and then
spend the rest of their working lives in that profession. In the 1970s
the vast majority of people receiving the bachelor's degree must
seriously anticipate changing radically the nature of their jobs perhaps four, five, or six times during their working lifetimes. Each
change will require new skills, which frequently can best be developed by colleges. The techniques of instruction which worked for
sixteen- to eighteen-year-old children in the 1930s' middle classes are
proving inadequate for the needs of the young man of thirty who
has been a practicing engineer for seven years, and who now must
acquire the new skills of business management.

While a proliferation of knowledge was beginning to take
place in the 1930s, there was a relatively limited number of subjects, each possessing a logic of its own. The logic of history, economics, and political science was largely descriptive; the sciences
were typically presented in the curriculum by taxonomic botany
and zoology, chemistry, and physics; engineering concerned itself
with relatively straightforward problems of bridge and highway
construction, steel fabrication, and the like. The approaches and
logics of these subjects were relatively well known and understood,
but in the 1970s one sees the flourishing of new, hyphenated subjects attempting to bring together several logics which previously
were judged irrelevant one for the other, if not incompatible. The
pedagogical problems of teaching a sequence in bioengineering or
chemical physics or psychological economics require new ways of
presenting materials, new ways of comprehending large amounts of
materials, and, indeed, new epistemologies.

Again in the 1930s Oriental and non-Western lands were
rarely thought of, except by the "old China hands." Europe was
far away, but who ever heard of the multitude of little nations in
the Middle East? The cultural load of the college curriculum could
be Western European and North American in orientation. Foreign
languages were all basically Greek in origin, and lessons in geog-

raphy were quite circumscribed. Since those days revolutionary changes in communication and transportation have made the world shrink. The revolution of colonial peoples has presented the nation with new and perplexing tasks and the schools with the requirement to teach new and exotic languages, ideologies, and cultures. It is becoming obvious that the methods used for teaching French, with its heavy load of cognate words, will not suffice to teach the Vietnamese language.

Education in the 1930s was supported principally by faculty members who received inadequate salaries for their services, which they tolerated because college teaching was a comfortable existence. Endowments and reasonably limited state appropriations made up the bulk of the income of colleges and universities. During the 1930s, with the exception of a few institutions like Yale University and the University of Chicago, relatively little building was taking place, and colleges and universities could maintain a poverty-level solvency within which the prevailing modes of instruction did not seem extravagant. In the 1970s, however, the philanthropy of college teachers has all but disappeared. The cost of new buildings is causing states and institutions to waver at the number of students who want an education. Increases each year in total enrollment cost are at rates which some have feared might inundate the entire enterprise. In this context, it is apparent that older methods of instruction are too great an extravagance for even a wealthy nation like the United States.

Factors like these commend to colleges and universities the need to innovate. Such an injunction would be practically meaningless if there were no new practices and techniques to be adapted to the mission of higher education. But innovations are available: a rapidly expanding technology has produced equipment with educational potential and there are theories about better ways of helping people to learn. One of the purposes of this book is to suggest ways by which change can be engineered; a prior step must be to determine what activities are available for college teachers to use.

A few institutions and teachers, reinforced by limited research, are beginning to feel that students do not necessarily have to be in a formal classroom situation to learn even quite difficult subjects. It is becoming apparent that independent study has potential for students at all levels of collegiate education, not only for tailoring education to the individual student's needs, but for expanding the influence of significant professors. As we indicated earlier, the term *independent study* does not refer to the tutorial system which has been in vogue for over a century at Oxford and Cambridge. Rather, it refers to a student who selects a field of study or a particular project, receives some guidance from a faculty member, and then works on his own. An early formulation of this was the comprehensive examination system at the University of Chicago, which allowed students to study on their own and then receive academic credit on the basis of an externally prepared examination.

But there are other examples of independent study. Florida Presbyterian College freshmen have a period of independent study between the fall and spring terms. Ultimately, that college plans to have as many as 50 per cent of its students take the bulk of their four-year collegiate work by such a technique. Independent study can be found at the graduate level, where students take two or three methodology courses and then work on their own to broaden their understanding of a subject and to develop a research project. The students in the house plan experiment at Stephens College study the logic portion of a philosophy course during an intensive three- or four-week period of independent study. No formal instruction in logic is given. While an earlier inquiry suggested that independent study was enormously costly, the concept elaborated here need not be exorbitantly priced. The professor is expected to give some reinforcement and evaluation of the student's efforts, but the student himself is expected to fashion his work in ways which are consistent with his own personality and needs.

Technology has produced an amazing array of goods that have educational potential, of which television is the most obvious. Through open-circuit educational television Wright Junior College in Chicago offers credit courses to thousands of people in the Chicago area, requiring that the student come to the campus just twice, once to register and once to take a final examination. Even a final examination can be given over television, as an experiment at the University of South Florida established. At Stephens College, a closed-circuit television system allows a required course to be taught to an entire freshman class at the same time with no class having more than eighteen students. And at Stanford University, cadet teachers use television to view themselves in the act of teaching.

To television can be added tape recordings, filmstrips, and motion pictures, which can, if the instructor wishes, be linked into a multimedia program to achieve educational goals. A lecture given in the morning can be tape-recorded and placed on a continuous circle recording so it is available for several days. The telephone also has untapped uses. Institutions which cannot afford television equipment can be linked together in a conference arrangement through amplification systems, so that students from ten institutions can hear the same lecture and, through the telephone system, raise questions and respond to points the lecturer made.

Present levels of engineering allow a lecture podium to be equipped so that a professor can write on the podium and have the images conveyed to the entire class by means of an overhead projector. By activating another lever the professor can link his classroom into a television performance. Or with another control he can begin playing a film or a recording. When the instructor in this multimedia classroom calls for student response, the students push buttons on the arms of their classroom chairs and a modified computer immediately tabulates the responses for the instructor to see. Language laboratories can now allow a portion of a French class to listen to native speakers while another portion of the class speaks to the classroom manager or teacher and still another portion of the class uses a combination tape-book system to learn grammar.

The computer possesses pedagogical potential which is only beginning to be realized. At the University of Illinois an experiment allows a thousand students, each working on a somewhat different task, to speak to and obtain responses from a central computer. The computer system in East Palo Alto, California, allows disadvantaged children to work individually, either with a typewriter or an electronic light stick, to learn words and mathematical solutions at a faster rate than is possible in orthodox classroom settings. Medical students at the University of Missouri learn computer techniques for diagnosing illness and they improve their own diagnostic skills as well.

Of course, there are still more examples of technology. Relatively inexpensive dry-copying devices enable students to obtain library information quickly and then take it home with them, leaving the original document for other people to use. Specially equipped library tables allow students to tune in to music, commentary about books, or other prepared programs. Occasionally an entire institution combines technological devices into a whole new approach to education. One example is Oakland Community College in Oakland, Michigan, which serves approximately five thousand students on a campus with only three orthodox classrooms. The bulk of student learning is done individually in booths equipped with programed textbooks and tape recorders and small television viewers that are connected to a central pool of information.

Some theorists visualize the time when even individual homes would contain automated learning centers in which all members of the family could pursue important parts of their initial or continuing education without the need to leave home. Whether or not this is likely to be realized, the range of technological devices is surely great enough to pique the curiosity of professors who wish to try a new approach to a particular education problem.

But machines are not necessary for innovation. Breaking orthodox time patterns may enhance certain kinds of learning. A number of institutions moved from a semester or quarter system to a four-one-four plan, which allows students to take four courses in the fall and four more courses from the first of February until the end of the academic year. The previous dead time from mid-December until the end of January is converted into a short term during which students work on independent projects, travel, or do other things relevant to their educational program. Other institutions have adopted a three-three scheme, dividing the academic year into three equal chunks and asking that students take three courses during each of the three periods.

Still another modification intended to insure year-round utilization of physical facilities and allow students to proceed at varying rates of speed is the trimester system, first experimented with by the University of Pittsburgh, then by the Florida system of higher education and Parsons College. With the exception of Parsons, the trimester system has not resulted in heavy summer utilization of classroom space, but it has provided ways for students to accelerate their academic career. Institutions such as Antioch College and Northeastern University have for some time used a calendar which keeps a portion of the student body on campus engaged in orthodox academic work while another portion is off-campus, engaged in work related to their academic concentrations. The work is for pay and thus helps to defray some of the increasing costs of attending college.

Theoretical work done in the 1950s on space and faculty utilization indicated that no educational losses were suffered by asymmetrical scheduling of classroom space and time, and that the utilization of classroom stations was more efficient. In 1962 and 1963, the University of South Florida experimented with this scheme and discovered that it did, in fact, work. The university arranged classes into a variety of orders; a class might be held at 8:00 A.M. Monday, 10:00 A.M. Tuesday, and 4.00 P.M. Friday, for instance. Students and faculty adjusted to the scheme quite well and were satisfied with it.

A refinement of the asymmetrical schedule is a computer-based process of flexible scheduling, based on the idea that not all subjects or parts of subjects need the same amount of time from each student. By using the computer to make combinations, it is possible to put together a schedule for the academic year which will maximize use of space and follow student and faculty desires regarding the amount of time needed for each of a number of tasks. It may be that none of these time rearrangements is ideal for an institution, but since the academic year is not governed by immutable principles, experimentation is possible. Some institutions may wish to experiment with the single-course plan attempted in the 1940s by Hiram College, Chapman College, and Eureka College. Under this system students study one course for seven weeks, then shift to another. Other colleges may wish to have a long term in the fall, another long term beginning immediately after Christmas, and a short term at the end of the academic year. Still other colleges may wish to offer concurrently courses which last a semester, half a semester, or even a week or ten days.

Another cluster of innovations involves the sanctions, rewards, or punishments given to students in response to their educational performance. The grading issue has been lodged customarily in the relatively capricious hands of individual instructors and administered in the form of a five-point scale expressed as letters. Early modifications of the grading system resulted in grades being assigned by an external examiner, freeing the instructor to work with the student and not be in the position of judge. The honors program at Swarthmore and the examination system at the University of Chicago and Michigan State University were examples of this attempt. As the objectively scored examination movement gained headway, it was demonstrated that even quite abstract educational achievements could be measured by means of objectively scored tests.

Recent discussion has suggested that for some educational experiences a letter grade is not necessarily the most effective device. A written appraisal, conveyed to the student and placed on his permanent academic record, is one way of enriching grading. For other experiences perhaps no grades at all are appropriate. Students may avoid desirable but difficult courses in the interest of earning high letter grades. Allowing students to take at least some of their academic work in either a no-grade or pass-fail situation might encourage students to broaden their education. The premedical student might be stimulated to take a course in aesthetics if he knew that his predominantly number-oriented mind would not be penalized in dealing with a subject with a high concentration of abstract verbalism. Some students, disenchanted with orthodox courses in universities, engage in free university courses for which no grades are given. That these students still work diligently and gain quite a bit suggests that in some situations reliance on grades has been misplaced.

The Advanced Placement Testing Program of the College Entrance Examination Board makes refined placement of students in college possible. For some students, taking the college-level examinations can demonstrate competence in a number of courses, thus obviating the need for the student to enroll in formal course work. Students are thus not penalized if they take college-level course work in high school.

The cooperative work program idea began another range of innovations. This plan has been used experimentally by several institutions and it has received wide publicity. Its most visible expression is the increasing number of overseas experiences—a summer of travel abroad, a summer of study in a foreign university under the guidance of American professors, an academic year of study in a foreign institution, or a portion of a four-year career spent at a branch campus of the parent institution. In all these experiences, it is presumed that students gain value not only from seeing cultures other than their own, but also from a break in the sometimes monotonous procession of academic activities.

Foreign experience is not the only way to achieve some of these results, however. As we indicated previously, students could spend a portion of the year working on a geological survey or working in the inner-city ghetto for full academic credit. Unfortunately, some of these schemes bother college professors who believe that academic credit should only be given for certain kinds of activities. But the fact that even military service seems to result in some academic gains suggests that this reluctance should be reexamined. The point could be made by asking rhetorically which experience will leave the more lasting effect—a lecture course in urban sociology or six months in a Southern town organizing Negroes to vote?

Even the contrast of cultures can be emphasized within a relatively small geographic area. A psychiatrist teaching at the New School for Social Research made only one demand on the students in a course—that they penetrate a subculture substantially different from their own. The child from the upper middle-class, white, Protestant background who penetrated a Harlem Puerto Rican subculture gained more than he would have gained from spending a term and a half on one of the overseas campuses of Stanford University. It is encouraging to note that two merging midwestern institutions have substituted this subculture penetration requirement for traditional foreign language sequences.

While psychologists generally have offered few suggestions to improve the practice of education, as noted earlier, some are producing theory and evidence regarding possible innovative techniques. A Syracuse University experiment showed that an instructor in the social sciences who assumes a more dogmatic, authoritarian stance than do authoritarian students can force these students out of their authoritarianism into a more open attitude. A psychiatrist at Stanford has demonstrated that a reasonably well-adjusted person who is enthusiastic about something can move disturbed individuals toward a more healthy position just through the act of sharing enthusiasms.

Role-playing and psychodrama have been demonstrated to be reasonably effective ways of modifying attitudes toward inter-personal relationships, minority group members, and human con-flicts. For some conditions the sanction of punishment may be a necessary motivation for learning, but in most cases appropriate reward is more effective. This is probably the psychological principle undergirding the previously cited movement toward no grades. Some formulations of Jerome Bruner suggest that it is possible to develop, even in the quite young, a basic notion of the structure of a subject, and that once the structure has been assimilated, specific items or information is added to the individual intellectual equipment quite easily.

Jerrold Zacharias observes that in order to learn, individuals must have had the experience of trying to teach someone. He claims that some teaching experience is a necessary part of the program of every student, and this teaching need not be applied to a younger person. Young people, he finds, can teach older people with the same fundamental gains. The testimony of students who have taught disadvantaged or culturally different individuals in Project Oppor-tunity or the Peace Corps is additional strong evidence. Many of these suggestions are not yet well established by firm empirical test-ing. The point is that an examination of literature from anthro-pology, sociology, psychology, psychiatry, and physiology suggest new approaches for teaching.

Particularly in professional and technical education, specific skills such as surgical incisions, the manipulation of laboratory apparatus, administration of injections, treatment of architectural diagrams with silver compounds, and other technical tasks are better taught by mechanical devices than by lectures and physical demon-strations. Students can learn about a surgical procedure on a dog more effectively by watching a television presentation of the opera-tion than by watching the operation itself. For even quite compli-cated processes, a filmstrip with a carefully scheduled sound track is superior to a demonstration to a group, if for no other reason than that the student can use the filmstrip when he individually is ready to develop that skill.

A related innovation is the discovery that many things previously taught through direct student manipulation can be taught better by a demonstration. The chemistry department at the University of Kentucky became convinced that laboratory procedures for beginning chemistry could be taught more effectively through a well-contrived demonstration than by asking students to enter the laboratory—and there was an appreciable saving in glassware. In the biological sciences, Alfred Novak has demonstrated that what he calls "dry laboratory" experiences can frequently be more effective in developing experimental techniques, attitudes, and approaches. By dry laboratory he means that he presents a uniform set of data to a class and asks students to manipulate the data alone rather than to accumulate the data through actual lab work.

An important facet of innovation is the possibility that economies in the practice of education, rather than diluting the quality of education, can actually enhance it. Perhaps the first theoretical statement of this possibility came in the publication by Beardsley Ruml and Donald Morrison, *Memo to a College Trustee*. They argue that part of the high cost of undergraduate education stems from a proliferation of courses and the attendant decrease in the average size of classes. It is possible, they argue, for a liberal arts college to offer a few large-section courses, accompanied by a number of middle-sized courses and quite a few tutorial courses. Students would be assured a well-balanced undergraduate education and the income derived from the large-section courses, when spread over the full teaching responsibility, would allow fairly sharp increases in faculty salaries.

Earl McGrath followed this book with his *Memo to a College Faculty Member*. By analyzing the number of courses taught by different departments in fourteen institutions, he shows that quality is not related to the number of courses offered. Much-publicized Parsons College in Fairfield, Iowa, demonstrates that by limiting the number of courses in the curriculum and charging reasonably high tuition, it is possible for tuition income alone to pay quite high faculty salaries. Unfortunately, the Parsons experiment was contaminated by premature public utterances on the part of its president and because other parts of the institution's operation were allowed to fall into financial disarray.

Florida Presbyterian College anticipates that it will be able to compete for strong faculty persons and at the same time support its instructional programs with 85 per cent of the funds coming from tuition income. This is putting into effect a modified Ruml plan. It is even conceivable that such high-cost institutions as the major private universities could, by judicious pruning of curriculum, bring their financial houses into better order. Curriculum revision is just one area in which economies are possible, however. Mention has already been made of independent study as a means of stretching instructional resources, as well as a whole range of possibilities involving electronic media.

During the 1940s and early 1950s a number of programs in general education attempted to offer what were called interdisciplinary courses. Many of those interdisciplinary courses, however, were merely surveys of knowledge and opinion from a number of different fields. Today the research frontiers tend to be interdisciplinary in character and may suggest the rationale by which courses of a genuine interdisciplinary character can be provided. In a sense, the student demand for this type of course is implied in the request for free university types of courses.

One of the most pronounced trends in graduate education in the United States is an intensification of interdisciplinary doctoral programs. As these come into full being, a cadre of teachers will be prepared to offer interdisciplinary courses for the undergraduate population. If these interdisciplinary courses are widely adopted, the single-teacher system may give way at least slightly. One can visualize an undergraduate course on Florence of the fifteenth century taught by an art historian, a literary scholar, and a political historian. Such a team approach would increase the cost of education, but the cost of that rich sort of offering could possibly be offset by economies elsewhere.

The potential of interdisciplinary courses is clearly present, but there are major obstacles institutions must overcome. Although some deans of academic affairs anticipate a gradual erosion of the powers of subject matter departments, this is something for the future to reveal. Presently, especially in major universities, departments represent the strongest bastion of power and prestige, and departments typically do not throw their influence on interdisciplinary work. Faculty members, sensitive about their own professional futures, are inclined to stay with a single-subject department rather than to enter the somewhat dangerous ground of interdisciplinary work.

Several other sorts of innovation should be mentioned quickly. Long-range planning of services had not been generally practiced in American institutions until the end of the 1950s. However, the financial crisis which faced higher education in the 1950s and the anticipation of large increases in enrollment finally forced institutions to think about long-range fiscal and physical plant planning. When this process was undertaken, the absolute imperative that it be preceded by sound academic planning became apparent.

Thus, conditions today are hospitable to a thorough, conscientious, systematic pondering of the purposes of education, for the simple reason that this is economically sound. Within recent years, several large state systems of higher education have for the first time in their histories asked branch campuses to determine explicit long-term educational goals and make plans to achieve these goals. What was once the jargon of education—that is, the setting of educational objectives—has now become a respected and necessary act. The forty-seven-year-old School of Architecture at Princeton, for example, is using the theoretical constructs of curriculum analysis developed by Ralph W. Tyler to try to discover what should be the education of architects who will be practicing in the twenty-first century. It is strange that planning within a pragmatic society should be considered an innovation. Yet, so recent has been the validation of planning that it must be so considered.

During the late 1940s and 1950s, a number of institutions developed remedial centers and remedial programs. While some of the techniques did not actually work very well the remedial movement nevertheless demonstrated that not all entering students had the necessary preparation to do college-level work. Then in the middle 1950s higher education became concerned that the particular needs of the highly talented student were being overlooked as institutions directed their basic teaching at the middle-level student and

their specialized efforts at the marginal student. Thus began programs for the gifted: honors courses, honors degrees, and even honors
colleges. Once again, some of these efforts did not prove particularly
lasting, partly, one must assume, because they were not adequately
funded. A professor will work with honors students for a year or so
simply because he is interested in them, but unless he is rewarded
in the tangible things of his profession, he will not carry on these
activities for long.

Since the development of programs for the superior student,
colleges are becoming aware of other categories having equally discrete and unique needs. In the early part of the 1960s research
identified the creative person, who may or may not be the same
as the academically gifted person. Recently colleges have become
aware of the needs of the culturally disadvantaged students, and
are developing compensatory programs, enriched programs, and
programs involving specialized teaching methods in an effort to
help disadvantaged groups move into the mainstream of American
society.

Brief mention should be made of the innovations that are
possible through imaginative architecture. A few recently created
libraries—the Earlham College Library is an outstanding example
—are built on the idea that students do not like to study in large
groups at large tables. Thus, the library is arranged so that there is
no central reading room. Instead, study spaces and study chairs are
scattered throughout the library, giving a feeling of informality and
seclusion. In the past, one had the feeling that the size of some
sections of colleges was determined not so much by pedagogical
reasons as by the availability of space. Today architects are finding
that a variety of space sizes is needed, but that it is extravagant to
create such spaces in permanent form. Movable partitions and the
wise employment of carpeting (which allow a large, long space to
contain many different groups, each conducting its business without
disturbing the others) can provide this needed flexibility.

The possibilities of bringing learning and living together have
finally been apprehended and it is now deemed appropriate to place
learning spaces in residence halls. It should be pointed out that the
creation of new academic facilities which really do facilitate the
educational mission requires that faculty be involved in the plan-

ning. To do so, even though planning physical structures is a time-consuming process, is to gain another by-product, because faculty members are forced to spell out the kind of space they want and they must first determine the sort of educational program they propose to mount.

These, then, are some of the innovations in higher education which are possible. Quite probably there are others, but enough innovations have been suggested to underscore the point that approaches, techniques, and devices are available if faculty members will use them. The next task must be that of motivating faculty members to experiment.

VIII

Mechanisms
for
Change

We do not understand enough about how changes are effected in individual practice or in the nature of institutions to give definite, well-tested guidelines, but individual testimony and some observed institutional experiences suggest what ultimately may become elements of a theory of innovation.

Perhaps the most important element in effecting changed practice on the part of individual professors is for them to become personally involved in a movement which makes explicit to them the importance of teaching, the fact that others are concerned, and the fact that change is possible. In Florida, junior college teachers are brought together in workshops to discuss common educational problems and to plan experiments, which they evaluate in a workshop the following year. The Florida plan also allows faculty members from each of six institutions to visit all other institutions of the group, one each year, to allow an exchange of ideas. The Union for Research and Experimentation in Education sponsors a similar activity for individuals who come together for a summer workshop to plan an innovation, then are given the resources to conduct the innovation, and finally are brought together a subsequent summer to assess the experiment.

In the 1950s, the American Council on Education brought together representatives of each of six curriculum areas in general education programs from nineteen different institutions. For the most part, these representatives were classroom teachers with no particular expertise in tests, measurement, and evaluation. They participated in a variety of experiences, including summer workshops of one or two weeks' duration, short fall and winter meetings, visitation to campuses by members of the study central staff, and the organization of local committees. The work of the study was to make explicit the purposes of general education and to devise instruments by which the outcomes of general education could be assessed. The very act of attempting to do these two things indicated to a number of the participants that much of what they were doing in their classes was simply not relevant to the goals of general education.

The task of teaching is a difficult one, particularly since the results of teaching are so difficult to evaluate. Alone, an individual is likely to feel more secure engaging in a limited number of well-tried practices. But if a teacher can associate with others in a joint undertaking, he gains considerable strength and seems willing to depart from orthodoxy. This point about involvement can also be made negatively. The University of South Florida conducts orientation sessions for new faculty people. Evening meetings are held during the fall semester and such subjects as grading and the use of television are presented. For the most part, the sessions have not seemed very successful because the new faculty members felt it was something done to them rather than something in which they were involved.

The same institution also maintains an all-university committee on instruction which is charged with stimulating faculty members to think about new ways of teaching. Again, the committee has not been particularly successful because it appears almost as a wing of the administration seeking to do something to faculty members. The office or agency that desires to bring about change in method of instruction must contrive a situation in which individual faculty members become deeply involved, intellectually and emotionally.

This concept of contriving underscores the basic dilemma of college and university government. There is strong desire for a form of governance in which decisions are arrived at by consensus. Yet in practice there is, and very likely must be, a hierarchical form of government in which one element of the community is labeled administration and the other faculty. Within American higher education, the faculty has been inclined to be conservative about educational matters. The subjects taught are normally conservative subjects, keeping and recording important cultural information for the future. The division of college faculties into departments also contributes to conservatism. The administration, on the other hand, is the dynamic element, charged with exerting educational leadership. It is typically the administrative officer who hears of innovations and seeks to have them adopted on his campus. It is the central administration which must look at the total mission of the institution and then marshal the energies of the faculty to achieve that mission.

Thus the administration, the natural agent of change, is expected to contrive those situations which involve the faculty. The administration must make the strongest effort to keep the channels of communication unclogged and must seek to develop a consistent philosophy of education which can govern practice and establish parameters for programs.

Within the last few years a new administrative subspecialty has grown up on the campuses of the nation's colleges and universities. Florida Presbyterian College lodges in the academic vice-president responsibility for being the principal change agent. He views himself as a catalyst operating in an intensely political environment, his principal responsibility being to facilitate innovation in the educational process. The University of South Florida created a director of institutional research and a director of educational resources, both of whom are responsible for stimulating changes in education practice. In addition, the University of South Florida senses a responsibility for changing instruction in the state junior colleges. With outside financial support, the university organized activities designed to improve instruction both in the university and in a cluster of junior colleges.

The University of Georgia created an institute for higher education and assigned to it several innovation missions. It is to aid in the recruitment and training of new college teachers and to serve as the institutional research agency for the university. It facilitates cooperative work with other colleges in Georgia with a view to improving the training and the quality of teaching. It also maintains a comprehensive system which will provide institutions in the state with information that can be used for responsible decision-making.

The University of Michigan has created a center for the improvement of instruction and has staffed it with a number of psychologists, each of whom represents a different subspecialty. This center is assigned the mission of advising and assisting the university faculty in the improvement of instruction. The University of Tennessee created a learning resource center after a university committee realized the need for several different functions: research about teaching, dissemination of information about teaching to professors whose time normally was spent becoming more proficient in their disciplines, and stimulation of faculty experimentation with new educational approaches. A modification of the Tennessee center is the center for the improvement of instruction in mathematics and science at the University of Texas. The University of Kentucky and Oxford College follow more closely the pattern of Florida Presbyterian, and assign responsibility for innovation to the dean of the liberal arts college.

In the light of this premise regarding the role of administration, several guidelines can be suggested. First, an administration seeking to stimulate innovation should have a clear notion of the nature of academic government. One theory emphasizes four points: (1) that administrative authority, regardless of form or legal structure or both, consists of what is willingly delegated to it by personnel within the organization; (2) that the delegated body within this

organization of governments is the faculty, which functions respon-
sibly through representative channels and designated institutional
officers; (3) that the faculty is interested in assuming and coordi-
nating leadership and can be educated for such leadership and
cooperation; (4) that the end result of such a process is the
maintenance and enhancement of a productive morale—a condition
or attitude in which individuals in representative groups make
reasonable subordination of their personal objectives to the overall
objectives of the institution. The factors essential to such a condition
or attitude are feelings of mutual respect; a sense of common task;
a recognition of the role of politics, debate, understanding, and due
process; and the understanding that the basis of good government
is ultimately the quality, character, and policy that exists in and
between the persons and groups within the government.

While such a statement concerning the nature of academic
governments assigns considerable responsibility to the faculty, it
does not detract in any way from the responsibilities and prerogatives of the administration. Consider several uses of one administrative prerogative. It may help for the administration to require as one
of the conditions of faculty employment that each faculty person
prepare a description indicating broad responsibilities and purposes.
Such an act not only helps a new teacher understand what he
should be doing, but the outcome also serves as a basis of periodic
evaluation of his progress. Thus, when a new faculty person joins a
staff, the written statement of his understanding of what he is to do
is placed in his confidential personnel file. At the end of the first
year, he has an interview with his immediate administrative
superior to discuss what he has actually done to implement the job
description. During the same interview, plans are made for professional development during the next year and again reduced to writing to be placed in his personnel file.

This yearly evaluation should be extended to cover other
pieces of evidence. If a college or university sincerely wants to make
changes in status on the basis of merit, then it should make a consistent and conscientious effort to evaluate as carefully as possible.
One technique is for each faculty member to be given a form on
which he indicates what he believes he has accomplished in the
classroom, on the campus, and in the larger professional world. He

can be asked to indicate what frustrations he has experienced, what he was unable to do, and what things he would like to do. At this level, it would probably be good to ask division or department heads to rank professors. This information should then be channeled to the next highest administrative office which, in the case of a small institution, might be the academic dean or, in the case of a larger institution, might be the dean of a college. Each professor should have his conference with this individual.

While evaluation of relevant activities is a powerful force by which administration can exercise leadership, there are others of equal potency. The manipulation of rewards, prerogatives, and perquisites is an important device. Greater use of individual independent study can be encouraged by paying a professor extra to offer such a course. Providing a faculty member with paid periods of leisure during the summer to allow him to prepare for an innovation is likely to be more productive than asking him to make the preparation on top of an already full schedule of teaching and scholarship. The catalogs of American colleges and universities are full of descriptions of programs for superior students or programs for independent study which are not operational because they were created as overloads on faculty members who did not receive commensurate remuneration.

Courses in general education have experienced difficulty retaining strong faculty people primarily because the problems of the reward system were not accurately analyzed. Within the American system, as has been indicated, rewards have been associated with departments, subject matter, or discipline-related activities. It is through the department that the person publishes, receives outside financial support, and establishes his professional reputation. To ask a person to teach an interdisciplinary course is to ask him to divorce himself from his secure source of rewards. Unless the institution secures compatible rewards for the new activities, one can predict that the new activity will not be particularly attractive. One institution, in recognition of this problem, has a sabbatical leave policy which allows a person who develops a new course in general education to take his sabbatical leave at the end of three years rather than at the end of six.

Numerous minor rewards can encourage faculty to be innovative, or at least intellectually alert. The provision of adequate clerical services, authorization of reasonable travel funds, institutional purchase of journal article reprints, and attention of the full institution to notable achievements are all illustrative. Even such a small thing as an administrative officer going to a faculty member's office rather than calling the faculty member to the central administrative building can develop rapport which can be a potent tool to stimulate faculty motivation to change.

The administrator who is willing to make faculty members truly responsible for the consequences of decisions about their own affairs also illustrates good administrative practice. During the time when the state of Michigan was experiencing a severe financial crisis, faculty members of one of the tax-supported universities in that state were given the largest salary increases in the history of the institution. The university received no increase in appropriations but anticipated and experienced a substantial increase in student enrollment. The dean of this college gave his faculty the choice of devising ways to accommodate increased enrollment with no additional staff but with increases in average faculty salaries, or to keep the student ratio as it had been by adding necessary staff members with only nominal changes in salary. Under this stimulus, the faculty responded creatively and discovered that adding five persons to each laboratory section did not really spoil the whole concept of a laboratory experience in a natural science course.

As indicated earlier communication is essential, and sound, effective communication is a primary responsibility of college administration. Initial communication with faculty members takes place at the point of employment, and communication should proceed through various individual conferences over the years of a professor's service. But this is not enough. There should be written communication between the central administration, the faculty, board of trustees, students, and even parents. There might be voluntary faculty meetings in which no decisions are made but matters of a controversial nature are discussed. The administration could use social activities as a way of communicating. Even contriving a faculty caucus in which no administrative officers are present could be a way of unclogging channels of communication and ensuring greater freedom of expression. The point is that innovation is most likely to happen in an open society in which people know the things important to them personally and to the group of which they are a part.

Even a strong, imaginative college administration cannot operate without fully recognizing the enormous elements of power which do exist among college faculties. Normally, there will be a limited number of professors whom everyone respects and who possess controlling influence. To engineer change, the administration should make full use of such people, not only because it is politically wise but because it is a way by which a broad hearing can be given to innovative ideas. The general education unit of Michigan State University succeeded in large measure because the president of the university selected a key member of the faculty of the college of agriculture to chair the committee investigating general education, and then designated that same individual as the first dean. Associated with the dean were four or five of the university's outstanding scholars, who were asked to serve as department heads for the newly formed college of general education. The stature which these appointments gave ensured survival of the infant programs for at least a few years, and if they could survive that formative time, the likelihood was good for a long tenure.

The University of Kentucky funds a major self-study that created a broad new academic plan, initiated a new program of general education, began a systematic program of faculty evaluation with sanctions based on merit, and created a new academic organization designed to facilitate innovations. This all happened as a result of careful planning by a highly capable new president who sensed that there were strong elements of faculty influence upon which he could rely to bring about changes. Once these faculty members became convinced of the validity of new ideas the result of administrative leadership was a transformation of the University of Kentucky.

Innovation is not likely to come about unless the need is clearly perceived. A number of successful innovations are clearly traceable to the simple fact that a need had become painfully apparent. At Oxford College the majority of students were seriously in need of remedial work in language and mathematics. The faculty was aware of these deficiencies in basic academic skills, but did not

have the time to rectify them through orthodox ways. When programed textbooks and multimedia approaches to instruction became
available, and the faculty was shown the relevance of these new
devices for remedial work, an innovation was quickly accepted.
Without the stimulation of need, the faculty could have seen this
move as intensely threatening.

Michigan State University also was able to move to programed work in remedial mathematics when the widespread quantitative deficiency of the student body was generally realized, and
when the mathematics department realized that it was too small
to serve all of the functions expected of it. A handbook on improving
instruction and on the supervision of instruction succeeded when it
was directed specifically at the chairman and section leaders of large
multisectioned courses in a large institution. Had the same booklet been directed at the faculty generally, it likely would not have
had the same impact. Another booklet at the University of Michigan contains suggestions on improving instruction and seems to
have been well accepted because it is addressed to new faculty members. It contains a great deal of routine information, simply inform-
ing faculty members about how to make their way around that
complex campus. Again, there is a strong presumption that had the
booklet been addressed to the faculty generally the impact would
have been much less pronounced.

The previously mentioned workshop program involving
teachers in junior colleges and universities in Florida quite probably
has succeeded because both university and junior college people
realized how crucial it was that articulation on the curriculum exist
between the two levels. The University of Georgia program of
awarding predoctoral assistance valued at four thousand dollars a
year to faculty members from Georgia colleges is currently flourishing because the small Georgia institutions are striving mightily to
increase the proportion of Ph.D.'s on their faculties. They are willing to give young faculty members leaves of absence so that they
can complete doctoral work and at the same time be introduced to
new ideas about teaching.

Since uses of the computer are in vogue, a University of
Michigan workshop for faculty that shows how computers can be
used has been a successful venture from the standpoint of the num-

ber of people influenced and increased utilization of computer service. At the University of Texas a general questioning attitude within the department of chemistry concerning the nature of laboratory work in beginning chemistry provided the opening for a major change: separating the laboratory from the lecture course. By keeping the credit hours of both equivalent to what they had been, it became possible to eliminate laboratory work in chemistry for the nonscience major.

The significance of this point cannot be overemphasized. Until the 1964 events at the University of California, Berkeley, dramatized a need for a reappraisal of undergraduate education in major universities, the primrose path of increased emphasis on research and upper division and graduate work was being followed by most institutions with pretensions to major academic stature. The events at Berkeley and a few other institutions indicated that the time was ripe, that the need was present for a renaissance in undergraduate education.

Related to this matter of seeking innovation where the need is present is the principle of providing ad hoc assistance for professors as they develop their own ideas. At the University of Michigan a Wolverine Fund of $25,000 can be dispersed in small grants to help faculty members solve particularly vexing problems. This is not long-term assistance, but assistance for an immediate problem. A professor in architecture, for example, became discouraged at routinely teaching a procedure to each class of students. A small grant from the Wolverine Fund allowed him to develop a filmstrip and tape recording which could teach the process more effectively than a face-to-face confrontation, and could teach it when each student was ready to use it.

Short summer workshops, lasting from two days to a month, allow faculty members at Stephens College to work on small problems which have plagued them and which they have been unable to find sufficient time for during the normal academic year. An office interested in building influence as an agent of change would do well to understand the areas of likely ad hoc faculty interest, and would be prepared to exploit expressions of interest on short notice. The new director of psychological services at the University of Georgia Medical School spent the first eight months of his appointment just familiarizing himself with medical education, its problems, and the sort of difficulties faculty members might encounter in developing innovative ideas.

A major device for facilitating change in college teaching, which by no means has been perfected, is to gain the support of people whose primary obligations and loyalties are with academic disciplines. Within the academic system, faculty members think of themselves not as teachers in a generic sense of that word, but as historians, sociologists, chemists, and the like. It is only when they can see that an innovation helps—or certainly does not hinder— their functioning in discipline roles that the innovation is attractive.

Many different methods to link the disciplines with peda- gogical innovation have been attempted and some have been success- ful. The American Association for Higher Education met with representatives of the learned societies and formed an ad hoc com- mittee which took as its first task the preparation of a unique book. The first portion, prepared by an eminent psychologist, indicated basic learning principles; the second half was prepared by respected practitioners in each discipline. Thus there would be a handbook for historians, another for sociologists, and still another for philoso- phers. It was hoped that this aura of respectability would make the book on teaching acceptable to departments in large universities and in small colleges. Further, each chapter was directed at an area of need (multisectioned courses, for instance) so that the book could not threaten senior faculty members convinced that their own techniques of teaching were eminently sound.

Florida Presbyterian College has managed to gain wide acceptance for independent study, partly because faculty members were shown how undergraduate students could be associated with them in their own research undertakings, with respectable results. The fact that a piece of work done by a freshman in chemistry was published served as potent evidence to the discipline-oriented faculty that a new wrinkle in pedagogy could be respectable from a sub- ject-matter point of view. The fact that all professional staff mem- bers in the University of Michigan center for the improvement of teaching are psychologists and that all have appointments in appro- priate academic departments in the University makes the rest of the faculty more likely to seek the services the center can render. The senior author has had considerable experience consulting with liberal arts college faculties about improvement in instruction, and he is convinced that one reason his suggestions have sometimes been followed is that his education is in the field of history.

The University of Texas maintains a small center for the improvement of instruction in mathematics and science. The center's greatest impact is gained from the fact that its advisory committee is composed of faculty members from a number of departments, and that those faculty members are distinguished scholars. Certainly the fact that Jerrold Zacharias was a distinguished physicist made possible national acceptance of the need for a revision of secondary school physics courses.

Since faculty members in schools of education are professionally concerned with the process of education, they should be an important resource to help college faculties improve their teaching. But schools of education have been preoccupied with the problems of elementary and secondary education, and they have been inclined on occasion to overelaborate the obvious, so that they have alienated themselves from the processes of education on the college campus. The principle, then, is that efforts to stimulate innovation in a college or university should be related in no organic way to a school of education. The agent for change should be able to use relevant resources from a school of education, but the effort itself should be lodged elsewhere. Hopefully, this condition will change as strong departments or schools of education develop respected centers for the study of higher education.

The use of the "sociological stranger" is of considerable importance. The sociological stranger is one who is familiar with an institution, yet is apart from it. One of the earliest expressions of this concept was at Stephens College in Columbia, Missouri. The dean of education at the University of Illinois, W. W. Charters, was designated director of research on a part-time basis at Stephens. He went to the campus several times during a year to consult with individual faculty members, listen to their problems, suggest experiments, or point out things to which the institution should give attention. By establishing deadlines he would create motivation for action when he left. On his return to the campus he would find out what had happened. He had reasonably high status and reported directly to the president, but he had no administrative responsibility and could fire no one. He was a person of great personal integrity, and he could look at the institution more objectively than could the people who were there every day.

This role requires more than just a one- or two-day visit of a consultant, although consultants' services can be of value. The role of the sociological stranger requires that the person be familiar enough with the institution to identify areas of need, sense readiness for innovation, and be able to tap the resources to bring it about. An institution that makes use of this device should consider contracting with someone for a period of at least four or five years. A first visit of several months on the campus would help the stranger know and be known. Visits of about five days' duration three or four times a year should then suffice.

Consultations of one or two days at a time also have value. Frequently the observations of a person from some distance away will be more readily accepted than observations made by persons on the campus itself. An administrator may know well where innovation is needed and the source from which it should come, but the suggestion for a new calendar, a new method of teaching, or even a new course often comes better from the mouth of an outsider. If the outsider comes from a distinguished sister institution, so much the better. Of course, bringing in a consultant can be dangerous. It is possible that the consultant's ideas are not as well known by the administrator as he thought they were, and a visit from such a consultant could build up an effective counter-force against innovation. A relatively small cadre of people have successfully played the role of consultant or sociological stranger.

Outside forces and agencies can also be used to bring about change. The United States Office of Education, with its financial resources ready to support innovation, is one source; but even state legislatures can fulfill this role. Oregon State University, at the prodding of the legislature, is looking at the improvement of undergraduate teaching. The legislature appropriated one-half million dollars to be distributed in increments of one thousand dollars over a biennium to undergraduate teachers. Several Oregon institutions rejected this move as legislative interference with academic freedom

—that is, legislative judgment in what is essentially a professional matter—but several other Oregon institutions did accept funds. The institutions now have the responsibility of selecting faculty members each year who will receive the awards.

The Oregon State climate was modified considerably during the first year of operation of that program. For twenty years Oregon State students had used an optional teacher evaluation form. During these twenty years the highest number of forms used in any one year was fifteen thousand, and a normal year's use was between six and seven thousand copies. During the first year the rewards were offered, twelve thousand copies of the evaluation form were used in the first term and seven thousand more forms were used in the second term; fifteen thousand more copies were ordered for use during the spring term which, incidentally, was the term in which the selections were to be made.

It can be argued that legislative action did stimulate the faculty to think seriously about teaching, so much so that faculty members who never before had used evaluation devices were trying to get insight into their own practices. Accreditation agencies have been used in a similar way: a visiting committee exerts pressure that those on campus who are concerned with innovation are powerless to exert. Foundations, alumni bodies, organized parent groups, and organized student groups are potential forces for change. Clearly, there are dangers. The American university prides itself (unrealistically, we should add) on the fact that it stands independent of the rest of society. Actually, colleges and universities stand as service agencies to society and must be responsive to its needs. When society finally does express itself, institutions and their professional faculties may have to respond or lose their viability.

For over twenty years the North Central Association has conducted a study of liberal arts education which is really a device to help about eighty colleges improve themselves. This outside force facilitates communication and stimulates innovation through workshops, campus visits by consultants, and special projects, one of which has particular relevance here. Eight colleges in Kansas agreed to try to improve instruction through a research study. Using a method called the critical incident technique, judgments about effective teaching were obtained from two thousand students. The survey simply asked students to tell something a teacher did within the past two-week period which was effective and something which was ineffective. All these incidents, when classified and categorized, helped the faculty see themselves as students saw them.

A vast amount of information about higher education and its practices is becoming available. Research pours from centers for the study of higher education. Professors of higher education are focusing doctoral studies on the college enterprise. Members of other disciplines are doing research on higher education. Institutional research offices are producing information, as are such para-educational agencies as the Educational Testing Service and the College Entrance Examination Board. This literature is approaching flood stage, but much of it has relevance for an individual faculty member seeking to innovate. The question arises, How can the relevant information be brought to his attention?

One important mission which the centers for the improvement of instruction see for themselves is the dissemination of information. Generally they publish news bulletins, letters to the faculty, or brochures which describe what is going on at the local campus or elsewhere that might be of interest to deans and faculty members. For several years at Stephens College and at the University of South Florida a brochure distributed about every three weeks summarized research studies of interest to the faculties of these two institutions. Both the University of Michigan and the University of Tennessee publish similar brochures, each one of which, however, deals with but a single topic.

Written dissemination is probably not enough; there is room for the informal faculty meeting or bag-lunch meeting at which interested faculty can be informed of new developments. There is also room for the institutionwide, statewide or even regionwide conference to acquaint faculty with what is new in teaching. One of the important roles performed by the annual Conference on Higher Education is communication. The need for more information, written in capsule form, lies behind the development of *The Chronicle of Higher Education*. The United States Office of Education series, *New Dimensions in Higher Education,* has proven of considerable value and the Office is now considering several intensive searches of the literature to bring the college teaching profession up-to-date information about developments.

One important tool for motivating an institution to change is an institutional self-study. Part of the regeneration of the University of Kentucky came from a massive self-study, which then became the basis for an equally massive academic master plan. Stanford University shifted its character from that of a strong regional university appealing to bright, wealthy, underachieving students to a university of international stature primarily as a result of the findings of a self-study. Stephens College undertook a self-study when its administration believed that the time had come to minimize the traditions of an earlier era. That self-study was used to loosen the soil of academia so that a new president could have a reasonable chance of exercising academic leadership.

Occasionally self-studies have an opposite effect. Bowdoin College, for example, after conducting a Ford Foundation-supported self-study, reported its finding in a booklet entitled *Education in the Conservative Tradition*. The central thesis of that report was that virtually everything going on at Bowdoin was good and that there was no reason to change. But if a self-study utilizes a large segment of the faculty and inquires into all parts of the institution, it can become a significant vehicle for change.

A last guideline is simply a restatement of the aphorism that nothing succeeds like success. The faculty at Oxford College looked more readily at multimedia devices when it was demonstrated that student deficiencies in academic skills could be rectified by using automated self-instructional devices. Some faculty at the University of Tennessee approved a policy of allowing any course to be taken by independent study when it was demonstrated that certain students achieved more by not attending class than by facing the teacher. Florida Presbyterian College was able to expand independent study throughout the four-year college period and to a larger number of students when it was demonstrated that freshman students could do creditable independent work during a five-week intersession. Nursing schools embraced such aids as filmstrips and tape-recorded instructions when it was shown that nurses who learned administration of a hypodermic needle with an orange, filmstrip, and tape were more proficient than nurses who were given

instruction by an instructor. This leads to the significant point that
evaluation methods should be built into every effort to innovate.

From these broad guidelines it is possible to derive several
principles, which are advanced so that they can become categories
in an emerging theory of engineering for change. The first principle
is that vigorous, strong, and occasionally ruthless administrative
power is necessary, because in America faculties are essentially conservative, while administrative officers are essentially dynamic and
creative. If an institution lodges too much power in the faculty, the
institution dies; innovation does not take place.

When the administration is too strong the results are also
destructive: the sheer rapidity of change can shake the institution
to pieces. If one accepts the reality of this construct, that is, one
power valence in the hands of faculty and another in the hands of
administration, then it is possible to seek ways by which these two
forces can be brought into positions of creative tension. Out of this
creative tension can come innovation, but it must be tempered by
a knowledge of how much innovation the institutions can stand.
Through formal organizational assignment of powers, some to the
faculty, some to administration, it should be possible to achieve this
system of academic checks and balances.

The second principle is that all human beings, including
faculty members, are sufficiently venal so that it is possible to purchase interest or loyalty. Through financial incentives, free time,
and perquisites, it is possible to move faculty members from a preoccupation with limited concerns to interest in pedagogy and the
broader problems of education.

The third principle is that leadership for innovation can be
exerted by almost anyone. A person does not really need to have
a high-sounding title in order to exercise considerable leadership.
In its formative years, the University of South Florida maintained
a combined position of director of testing and director of institutional
research. The first incumbent was a fairly aggressive individual who
began to interest himself in a wide range of institutional concerns.
The report of a trial visit from the Southern Association during the
first year of the university's operation emphasized how much leadership that one officer had achieved. The report stated, "Things are
going fine, but we advise you, Mr. President, to have care lest an

office such as the office of testing and institutional research become too influential in the institution." A reasonably aggressive person lodged someplace in the institution can become a leader for change simply "by putting the saddle on his own back."

The fourth principle is that improvement requires time. One can speculate that college professors do not teach better than they do because they are inclined to impose on themselves, or have imposed on them, impossible time schedules. The faculty work load is improving, yet in junior colleges and some liberal arts colleges teaching loads extend from twelve to fifteen hours a week divided into four or five courses. Given the present rapid rate of increase of knowledge, few college professors are sufficiently intelligent or cosmopolitan to teach five or six different courses at the college level over a two-year period, and the sheer struggle to stay abreast of knowledge prevents innovation. The point is that if an institution wants innovation and improvement, time must be provided.

The fifth principle is that innovation is likely to be encouraged if the institution develops a sufficiently refined system of cost accounting so that actual costs of instruction as presently performed are revealed. If instructors could be shown the high cost to themselves personally of the small, inefficient courses taught by lecture techniques, one can speculate that changes in the curriculum would come about quickly. If cost accounting could show economies from the use of independent study, from television, or from other innovations, faculties would be more likely to accept them.

The sixth and last principle is based on an assumption that many faculty members are threatened and insecure individuals. Change is threatening, and an insecure person reacts defensively to threats. The officer or agency for change must build into the planning a provision for alleviating faculty anxiety and insecurity. It is almost possible to argue that this is so significant that institutions could well provide psychiatric services for faculty members, chargeable as a legitimate expense to the instructional budget. If a faculty person is relatively tranquil within himself, he can be expected to be relatively tranquil in examining a revolutionary new idea. If, on the other hand, he is anxiety-ridden and concerned about his status, he will reject anything which may change his status.

Clearly, these suggestions are based upon limited experience. Broad theoretical formulations are needed, as well as more experiments and field testing. Hopefully, some of the new centers for the improvement of teaching will attempt to provide additional information.

IX

Teaching
for
Students

Since education depends on teachers and their responses to students, the demands for new educational experiences will entail substantial changes in teacher behavior. These changes are likely to be of the same magnitude as those introduced when the colonial college felt the impact of the German university tradition. Before this impact, the prevailing style of education was recitation and rote learning from classical authors. Then, the lecture and seminar methods imported from Germany required different aims and skills from teachers: a moderately well-trained tutor could handle a recitation but could not function well in the freer discussions of a seminar.

This is not to say that earlier styles of teaching were invalid

129

or irrelevant to educational needs. The recitation system of instruction was highly appropriate at West Point in the early nineteenth century, for it did ensure that every cadet was actively involved in each subject every day. The lecture method was a way for a research professor to present his findings before they were published in less perishable form. Conditions, however, do change, and they have changed sufficiently in the last half of the twentieth century to require substantial changes in teacher behavior.

Lecturing as it is currently done seems less necessary because other sources of information are available. At one time a mathematics professor could believe that, all things considered, it was better to lecture and place his proofs on the blackboard. Now the easy availability of rapid duplicating techniques suggests that the mathematics lecturer might hand students copies of a number of proofs and spend his time explaining the theory behind them. The rapid spread of the paperback book industry, with ready anthologies, books of readings, and monographs, and the transmission of information through mass media minimize the information function the formal lecture filled. And even if the professor does need to present orally information not available elsewhere, he can tape-record or videotape his presentation, and students can listen when it is important to them to hear what the professor has to say.

Several institutions, such as Oakland Community College, the Miramac campus of St. Louis Junior College District, and Oklahoma Christian University, have extensive files of lectures on tape. Students can turn to these tapes at their convenience, which obviates the need for students and faculty to confront each other three or four times a week for the professor's lecture. This minimized need for lecturing seems especially marked in selective institutions, which attract students with high verbal ability who can obtain information in other ways more readily than by listening to a professor. For example, when Antioch College developed its freshman year program, which allowed students to obtain information in a variety of ways, attendance at lectures fell off drastically but there was no loss in information learned.

Then, too, students are critical of the lecturing skills and styles of many of their professors. The transmission of information through a lecture requires a high sense of syntax and language

structure and considerable physical and mental animation. Too frequently the professor offers neither.

Professors in the past have insisted upon a number of requirements to control students. Students were required to attend
class, but this control was reluctantly yielded as institutions faced
the reality that students might do something other than attend class.
Schools then created cut systems. Faculty members have insisted that
they should grade so that they could coerce students into doing the
necessary homework. This is well illustrated at the University of
Chicago, Michigan State University, and the University of South
Florida, all three of which at one time maintained a comprehensive
examination system which delegated grading to an agency other than
the professor. The theory was that if professors did not grade, students and professors could work together in greater harmony. However, in each of those institutions professors exerted successful pressure for the right to assign part of the grade as a coercive tool.

In view of current student desires for freedom and the fact
that many students, especially those in highly selective institutions,
have academic aspirations before coming to college, such requirements as grades and class attendance appear increasingly unimportant and even onerous. Even in professional schools the coercive
power of grades seems less necessary, and several institutions, such
as the law school of the University of California, Berkeley, for
example, have turned to a simple pass-fail method of assessment.

It should be pointed out that as class attendance and grading techniques are minimized, professors often feel insecurity and
uneasiness at what they consider wrong student decisions. For
example, in the 1967-68 school year, Wesleyan University abolished
all course requirements, allowing each student to select those courses
which in his judgment and that of his adviser made most sense. This
decision has been accompanied by a drop in enrollment in science
courses by nonscience students. This bothers scientists who believe
that a scientifically based society should ensure that all future
judges, writers, and legislators have some understanding of science.
Some teachers have contemplated restoring regulations, but another
alternative is open: to ponder whether the science courses as they
are currently conducted repel all students except those who must
take them for certification. There is evidence to show that students

can handle freedom and perform in ways equal to their performance under a more coercive system.

Today, teacher-dominated discussions seem no more defensible than teacher persistence in lecturing or establishing prescriptive requirements. In one graduate seminar, the senior author decided to make only one presentation during the full term and then to allow each student to report on a major domain of research and collateral efforts. The end-of-seminar assessment indicated that students believe this to be a highly effective means of education, especially since they were assuming the initiative in interpreting research findings rather than having the professor impose such interpretations. Here we see that student needs and desires are frequently at variance with those of the professor. If the professor structures a discussion, it will proceed in the light of his goals; while there could be some value in this for students, it appears that shifting more of the initiative to students would do more to help them grow.

College faculties might well examine some of the literature from counseling and psychotherapy which shows the values to an individual of conversations rooted in his concerns rather than the concerns of the therapist. This is not to suggest that classrooms become therapeutic sessions. A patient approaches a therapeutic session with much more acute concerns than he normally will in a classroom. Yet some of the values of nondirective therapy seem consistent with what students expect and would like to receive from their college classes.

There is evidence that students actually do fashion their own curricula and use instructional resources for their own ends, complying with instructor-imposed organization only out of superficial etiquette. The earlier cited Becker study of medical students is strongly indicative of this phenomenon. Also suggestive is the young student who listened many times to a single tape recording of a professor's lecture, but who did not attend any formal lecture. The student managed to improve the quality of his poetry to his satisfaction, even though the professor felt personally hurt and somewhat resentful when the student was not physically before him.

The increasing age of college students and their assumption of many adult roles without complete adult status suggests that the subtle relationships between professor and student also must change.

Students do want some close relationship with at least a few professors, but they would like to feel more equality and respect than presently exist. Professors undoubtedly gain psychological satisfactions from maintaining a master-disciple relationship with students, with the implication that students are really inferior. But this is not what students want. They want help in becoming fully autonomous individual adults, and they expect to be regarded as respected individuals well along the way in that quest.

The next matter is an ambivalent one. On the one hand it seems clear that students will no longer tolerate institutional or professorial regulation of their personal lives or personal conduct. Thus, what a student wears to class, what he does outside of class, how he conducts himself in the residence hall, and the like can be of no direct concern to his teachers. This implies that colleges and universities are moving toward an exclusive interest in the academic or the intellectual and away from any interest in education of the whole man. And, in the sense of denying rights to regulate, this implication is probably true. However, the full range of personal behavior can be open to professorial influence through educational devices, provided, of course, that individual students wish this to happen.

On the other hand, students are asking that the college experience far transcend a preoccupation with the academic and the intellectual. In the past there has been a tendency for professors to view what happens to students in classrooms, libraries, and laboratories to be the real life, and what happens outside to be a distraction and dilution of what is important. Colleges assign less stature to students' educationally related off-campus activities than to classroom work by the simple device of not granting academic credit. Thus, field trips during an interim term or a summer session are tolerated and sometimes provided, but there is reluctance to grant academic credit for them. Students are interested in moving back and forth between the academic world and what they see as the real world, and professors must accept the educational validity of this interest.

There is evidence that in spite of strong democratic pretensions, colleges and universities in the United States are the most authoritarian, autocratic institutions that society supports. The power of professors over students has existed almost without challenge since the beginning of higher education. In this country professors can assign grades on whatever basis they choose, and in the past there has been no appeal open to students. Professors have prevented students from graduating simply because of what the professor felt was contumacious behavior, and this power has been upheld in court. By refusing to accept a doctoral thesis a graduate professor has the power to alter an individual's entire life, and professional courtesy restrains colleagues from even questioning such actions. Professors have been allowed to decide who could and could not enter their own classes, sometimes through a system of stated prerequisites but frequently on a personal basis. This treatment was tolerated on grounds that the professor as a professional knew best and could be challenged only by his professional peers.

This power, however, is gradually being eroded through court actions and to an increasing extent through student resistance to professorial capriciousness. Behind student demands for a pass-fail system of assessment stands the clear awareness of how whimsical and frequently vindictive the five-point grading system is. Professors adapting to the new and freer curriculum must assume that arbitrary exercise of power over elements of students' academic life must cease as institutional power over students' private lives is disappearing.

Much of academic practice has been based on what might be called a psychology of poverty. This point of view holds that each individual's potentialities are limited through genetic or environmental influences, and that an important task of education is to screen out those individuals who had reached their own potentiality. College admissions procedures are premised on finding those students who can survive academically and excluding all others. The use of the normal curve of distribution with a stable percentage of students who will fail is rooted in the same interest in survival. The president of the state university who, when addressing the entering freshman class, told students to look carefully at the persons sitting to their immediate right and left because by the end of the year one of those two would be gone from the institution was articulating the prevailing belief in the college as a screening agent to remove the unfit. It was this attitude which led the highly selective institution to be almost completely segregated, because few from the culturally disadvantaged groups in the country—whether they were Puerto Rican, Negro, rural New Englanders, or people from the farms and hamlets in Appalachia—could demonstrate the same potential ability as students with higher cultural backgrounds.

Gradually, institutions have been forced to modify admission standards, and professors have been led to rethink their stance regarding low student performance. Indeed, professors in at least a few institutions have taken the position that failing students is as much an indictment of the professor as of the student, and they have adopted a policy of issuing no failing grades. Students are expected to persist in a course until they have demonstrated adequate competence or until they have decided to shift to some more congenial study.

Professors will be expected to change their ideas about standards. Before World War II, most tax-supported institutions were required by law to admit any high school graduate, and most of the private institutions accepted the large majority of candidates who applied for admission. The tremendous increase in the number of potential students after World War II, the greatly increased interest in the values of higher education, and the lack of space allowed undergraduate institutions to become more selective along the limited dimensions of measurable verbal or mathematical aptitude. This allowed prestige institutions to shift from a posture in 1952 of admitting one out of every two students who applied to a practice in 1965 of admitting one out of every eight or nine who applied.

However, there is no good evidence that this high selectivity is producing any more effective human beings than did the earlier, less selective approach. Nevitt Sanford, reflecting on Berkeley, recalls that in the 1950s almost anyone who had received a bachelor's degree could be accepted into graduate school, and, once accepted, if he had the perseverance he could obtain a Ph.D. If a student ran into obstacles on his oral exams or dissertation, the graduate faculty would work with the student, stretch their own notion of standards, and finally pass him. Now the institution is highly selective, and faculty members talk a great deal about maintaining appropriate standards. But Sanford doubts that those who are now receiving Ph.D.s under these high-pressure conditions will be more able or creative than those produced in the 1940s or 1950s.

Professors adapting to curricula based on developmental needs of students must alter their ideas about standards, and when they are concerned about maintaining standards faculty must base them on broader considerations than the students' simple ability to succeed in academic work. It also seems clear that institutions must reduce requirements and regulations for students. As this happens, professors will find themselves teaching in something which could resemble a free market situation where students will have choices. It seems patently clear that if a free election system with guidance should emerge, faculty members will be forced to respond to competition through some means other than political manipulation within the faculty to ensure appropriate enrollments.

As professors ponder changes in teaching styles, they can find suggestions of student expectations in recent studies. Undergraduate students seem to enjoy knowing about and being involved in the professors' own scholarly work. However, students are inclined to reject being forced to listen to professors' reminiscences about their personal lives. The students in the freshman-year program at Antioch College, when freed from formal course requirements, tended to stay away from the formal lectures and structured classroom activities. However, they would flock to hear a professor talk informally about his own research and to discuss with him the implications for human life deriving from that research.

Several problems emerge if this expressed interest of students is valid. If students are to be involved in this informal association with professors' scholarship and research, time must be rearranged for this to happen in a natural rather than a contrived way. This would require a reduction in time assigned to formal activities, so that both faculty members and students would have a sufficiently flexible schedule to come together when student needs arose. For instance, a student load might be divided into three parts. To satisfy two of these parts, students would enroll for formal courses. The third part could be satisfied through a variety of informal ad hoc experiences varying in length of time and intensity. Similarly, a faculty load might be divided into perhaps four parts: two parts devoted to formal course work, one part for students in informal curriculur experiences, and one part for the faculty member's research or scholarship.

Students also seem to be saying that they wish to use the professor as an important resource when they need him and to be left alone at other times. They say that much of what is accomplished in formal courses could as well be acquired through reading or direct experience, or the rich store of audiovisual or programed materials. But from time to time they do need direct help and encouragement and they need to interact with a professor. Students in the Stephens College House Plan testified that the greatest value from the experience came from being able to see their professors in the afternoon when they wished to. Professors testified that being available was a substantial drain on their time and energies, but by rearranging the times for formal classroom work it was possible to accommodate the faculty members' personal and professional needs, the needs of students for formal experiences, and this casual, informal student-professor contact. Different institutions must approach this matter of flexibility versus structure in different ways, depending on the nature of the institution and its students. A residential college, which by its very nature imposes considerable structure, can be relatively free in modifying formal classroom activities. A commuter institution, which imposes no structure other than curriculum, however, probably cannot be quite so flexible since students appear to need not only freedom but some structure to give them security for pursuing intellectual activities.

Students also are saying that they would like professors to serve in part as organizers of experiences rather than as the prime providers of experiences. Thus to students, the professor who has spent a great deal of time organizing a syllabus, self-administered tests, audiovisual materials, workable bibliographies, programed materials for difficult parts of a course, and off-campus experiences is providing better instruction than the professor who gives information in lectures or in discussions.

It should be pointed out that not all students can tolerate the freedom to use educational resources at their own volition, and almost all demand greater professorial activity. At the University of Utah Engineering College, for example, several engineering courses were taught by providing students with a number of realistic problems which they were expected to solve in their own ways, using professional help only as they felt they needed it. About half of the students enrolled in these experimental courses were highly pleased and demonstrated through tests that they had acquired the necessary skills and information to master the course. The other half, however, suffered increased anxiety throughout the semester and frequently asked professors to resume lecturing to give them the needed information for a bachelor's degree in engineering. The same student reactions occur in experiments with what might be called nondirective teaching. When the professor tells a class that it may consider anything its members wish to and in any ways sensible to them, a portion of the class will fashion a curriculur experience which is psychologically related to their needs. Other students, however, feel threatened and insecure at this lack of direction and become defensive and not infrequently abusive of the instructor.

Theoretically, it should be possible to appraise in advance students who can and cannot adapt to freedom and flexibility, but unfortunately this does not seem to be the case in American colleges or universities. The history of neglect of such information as scores of academic aptitude tests does not suggest that more sophisticated screening along dimensions of personality variables would likely be used. Rather, a combination of structured experience and unstructured time might be developed with the proviso that those students able to function alone should be allowed to do so. In a formal course, for example, these adaptive students would feel free to attend class or not and would not be penalized if they chose something other than listening to their teacher.

While students do not seem to want intimate contact with many professors, they testify that they face many critical decisions and need adult help in making them, but they want that adult help to be precisely knowledgeable. Students seem to be saying that they wish to find a professor from whom they could obtain precise information and with whom they could talk over basic questions about curriculum choices, careers, marriage, and their own identity. Repeatedly they emphasize that they do need a parent surrogate at times, while at other times they want to be independent of this parentlike figure. What they resent is the professor who seeks to exercise all the prerogatives and powers of parents all the time. The responsibility of being on call when students want guidance probably is difficult for a majority of professors to assume, for professors themselves have basic psychological needs. Yet those needs should probably be sacrificed for the needs of students if professors are going to serve in a helping profession. There should be other compensations for this sacrifice.

These points are well illustrated by a paraphrase of what a number of students said[1] at the National Conference on Student Stress in 1965:

We don't want protection. We want a chance to think for ourselves about politics and morals, and how we can earn good livings but keep our integrity. What we get is a choice of a profession, with a lot of little packages tied to the thread that leads to medicine or business administration or engineering; and the packages are called philosophy and economics and what have you. They are too seldom geared to us and what we are; too seldom taught by people who want to find out about us; and too seldom informed by our efforts to make our needs known. We don't know how. That's one of the reasons we came to college, to find out, not to be filled up with facts and ideas that other people believe are important. We need relationships with teachers who will help us face the big, tough hang-ups: Am I a moral pacifist or a coward? Is abortion a humane answer to the problems of unwed motherhood? What has the pill got to do with my answer? Who am I? Where am I? Where am I headed? And do I really want to go there? Is an academic career any less sterile than one in business? What are the things that make a society really worth fighting for?

Evidence thus far might be construed to show that students are excessively preoccupied with individualistic concerns, that they are generally almost "loners." Such a conclusion would be unfortunate and untrue. Many students would like to engage in cooperative effort, not only with their peers but with their professors as well. One of the strongest advantages the students at the University of Utah saw in the problems approach to a course in engineering

[1] E. J. Shoben, Jr., *Students, Stress, and the College Experience* (Washington, D.C.: United States National Student Association, 1966).

mentioned earlier was the opportunity to work with faculty in solving problems which were realistic to students. When faculty members and students are brought together through such structures as a cluster college, a house plan, a team-teaching effort, and the like the group seems to develop a high esprit de corps and to enjoy enhanced development both of students and professors. The good relationships which a few graduate students have with their major professors seem to come from the opportunity for the student and professor to work together on something of interest to both.

This relationship can be terrifying for the professor who feels that only after diligent training in skills and after following a sequential series of problems are students qualified to address themselves to issues of importance. Rose K. Goldsen,[2] drawing on years of research at Cornell University, makes this point clearly:

The best students feel they are not being taken seriously, that they are being relegated to busy work and drudgery whose relevance to any serious educational purpose is by no means clear to them. The best students are talking about how they are alienated from the real intellectual life of the university. They say they want small seminars in their freshman and sophomore years, more personal intellectual interchange with their professors, more participation in curriculum planning and allocation of academic budgets. The best students, especially student leaders, are balking at what they say is irrelevant nonsense in the curriculum. . . . The students are asking for seminars, face-to-face contact with professors, personal attention. It is by no means clear that this is the best way to "train them up." (Some professors are at their best in such small seminars, responding to give-and-take; but others are much better delivering a prepared lecture, following an outline, talking clear up to the end of the hour without brooking contradictions or questions from students.) What is significant about the students' demands, and what must be taken seriously, is that they want to be "trained up." They want to be engaged in the professor's serious work, to have his serious attention.

    [2] R. K. Goldsen, "High Hopes and Campus Realities," in L. E. Dennis and J. F. Kauffman (Eds.), *The College and the Student* (Washington, D.C.: American Council on Education, 1966), pp. 117, 121.

They want to be used by him as an academic resource; they want to be put to work.

At the risk of some redundancy, some of the generalizations about new students as presented in the Hazen Foundation Report on students[3] are restated here to recall the background from which these new expectations of faculty behavior come.

(1) Students are seeking enduring commitments but are skeptical about the ideologies and orthodoxies that clamor for their loyalty. (2) Because of their suspicion about formal ideology, the new students turn to human relationships as the source of most of the purpose and meaning they seek in their lives. (3) The contemporary college student feels strongly the need to belong but is profoundly skeptical about most of the organizations he encounters, particularly an organization that claims to offer him an education. (4) The new student is generous and idealistic in his own fashion but is frequently fearful that any long-term commitment to social service may destroy his idealism and thwart his freedom. (5) The new students, for all their apparent poise and sophistication, are frequently hesitant and uncertain. (6) Because of his doubts about himself, about organizations, and the possibility of faith and commitments, the new college student has a tendency to be suspicious and distrustful of the administration, and to a lesser extent, the faculty of his college. (7) Students come to college with a great deal of excitement and willingness to do the work demanded of them, but their expectations and performance usually decline very rapidly during the first months of the freshman year. (8) Most students apparently expect that the college years will mark the definitive end of their dependence on their parents.

In these student expectations we find some assumptions to guide college teaching and advising. None of these are particularly new, yet they do depart from the implied postulates upon which much of contemporary college teaching is based. The first assump-

[3] *The Student in Higher Education,* report of the Committee on the Student in Higher Education (New Haven: Hazen Foundation, 1968), pp. 20–25.

tion is that students attending college have drives and urges which operate toward healthy development if given opportunity, encouragement, and freedom. Although the healthy development may diverge from professorial expectation, it is in the direction of individual autonomy and self-reliance. Too frequently, procedures such as regular lectures, attendance requirements, grades, assignments in textbooks, laboratory exercises, and specified dimensions for papers assume that without such prescriptions students will misuse time and resources and not use the educational opportunities open to them. Contemporary teacher behavior seems to assume that unless students are guided, learning will not take place. Particularly in the sciences and mathematics there is the feeling that unless students proceed sequentially, according to the logic which the instructor perceives, it will be impossible for students to understand the theoretical presuppositions of the science or mathematics.

But the argument here is that by the time an individual has reached postadolescence and has gotten into the educational process, he has values which will reinforce biological urges toward healthy development; and that if he has guidance when he needs it and freedom sometimes to flounder and to find consistent interests, he will use appropriate educational and growth opportunities. It is possible to conceive of a number of different sequential entries into mathematics according to individual flairs, styles, or interests. It is possible to conceive of one approach to the physical sciences which attempts first to inculcate principles and then later to show application, while another approach might be to enter science directly by reading science materials in the popular press. We know that one student feels the need to attend class daily while another wants to attend perhaps only once or twice during a full semester or even a year.

There is the argument that students from professional homes, strongly oriented toward intellectual activities and attending highly selective institutions, might be expected to profit from greater freedom, while students from a relatively low intellectual tradition attending an open-door junior college and faced with the competitive demands of academic work and a job could not. While institutional and student differences do suggest that perhaps different techniques should be employed, the underlying assumption can continue to operate. The Antioch freshman-year program provides one sort of freedom in a two-week orientation period and then relies on the students' judgment to select activities which appear worthwhile to them. At Oakland Community College a similar sort of freedom is allowed by providing students with a weekly motivational session followed by freedom to use the program materials and learning resources available in fully automated classrooms under the guidance of teacher-proctors. Both methods differ in essence from the style of education which requires students to attempt fifteen to eighteen classes a week, scheduled symmetrically, with the chief responsibility for assimilating materials resting with the instructor.

A second assumption is that learning is not necessarily logical but rather psychological, and it gets direction and energy from the learner rather than from the discipline. Such a proposition contends that while a subject or discipline may seem to have an order or logic, fundamentally that order is imposed by a human mind and that other human minds can impose a different but still effective order. One student might successfully approach the study of a foreign language through first learning grammar, while another could gain equal facility through the more direct method of reading materials having large numbers of cognate words, arriving at grammatical understanding only after he had developed considerable fluency. One student can comprehend the powers of science through probing one science, while another arrives at equal sophistication through browsing broadly in literature about a number of sciences. This is a particularly troublesome postulate for professors to accept if they have as individuals gained satisfactory achievement through a particular mode of inquiry. But each faculty member might be asked to reflect honestly as to how he managed his own development. If this question were answered, as many different styles would emerge as individuals answering the inquiry.

This assumption defends the validity of individual differences in learning. While it is assumed that a direct consideration of individual differences is imperative, we should remember how incomplete knowledge of the psychology of individual differences really is. At present "the liberation of individual potentialities remains largely a hope and a dream, while the networks of communication between the various individual islands are as yet blurred, and our first vague studies of group dynamics are so lacking in a clear communication theory relating to mutual liberation of unconscious dynamic components."[4]

The next assumption is that cognition and emotion are equally valid in the total human being and that each should be encouraged, cultivated, and expanded. There is a strong suspicion that college courses and college teaching have been excessively concerned with rationality and have nearly rejected feeling. Accordingly, courses in the arts are taught historically, with virtually no attention given to emotional response to the arts. Courses in the history of art are judged appropriate and studio courses are rejected on the grounds that they encourage dilettantism or superficial play. Actually, students cry for play and for feeling, but the way collegiate style has emerged, considerable guilt accompanies students who do give vent to playful or emotional behavior. This view undoubtedly will produce shudders in the orthodox academic man, who will argue that the academy has such a high responsibility for developing rationality and rational modes of inquiry that even to consider other factors would dilute the quality of education.

Gardner Murphy, however, provides an appropriate response to the extreme rationalist:

These thoughts suggest the parallel that the nurture of rationality may perhaps lie in other efforts than the sheer encouragement of rational thought; indeed, that the rational may best continue to grow in the instinctive soil in which it was engendered, and that too clear and sterile a surgical separation of thought from its ancestral and parental roots in love and impulse may threaten its viability. And, if this should by chance be true, it would mean that the learner must not be deprived of the riches of his impulse life, and that the teacher must be a quickener of that impulse life through which thought can grow, indeed, a shaper and molder of impulse into the rationality which comes from a healthy craving for contact with reality.[5]

[4] G. Murphy, *Freeing Intelligence Through Teaching* (New York: Harper and Row, 1961), p. 44.
[5] Murphy, p. 22.

A fourth postulate is that much human development takes place through the interaction of peers, and that for important learning the student peer culture is and must be of greater force than interaction between the younger and the older. The nature of the growth pattern of the human being makes considerable tension the rule in relations between young people and adults. From infancy the adult, capable as he is of granting or withholding from a child affection, love, and even life itself, has the child in a potentially threatening situation. As the child moves from home to school the teacher takes on many parental attributes. In the presence of a possibly threatening adult, the child or youth inhibits much of his natural curiosity for fear of alienating his powerful adversary. It may well be that much of the arid, moribund classroom work one sees in American colleges has its roots in the student's fear and resentment of the adult teacher. When almost all classroom work is conducted in such situations, the student's willingness and ability to learn may atrophy. Again, perhaps a wise and prudent blending of situations in which adults are present with situations where they are not present may increase learning possibilities in college education. Adults cannot abdicate the classroom because there are times when the students want and need their presence. On the other hand, there are important times when adults are really in the way. There really is a generation gap and this generation gap can be usefully exploited for educational purposes.

The corollary to this assumption is the idea that no one can really learn something until he has tried to teach it to someone else. Allowing or even contriving situations in which students teach each other may be the most important educational service a teacher can render his students. Such teaching-learning interaction among peers shows that cooperation and collaboration are good. Yet much education practice discourages cooperation or even penalizes it. Each student is expected to do his own laboratory work and prepare his own papers, although it is at least conceivable that greater educational gains would come from cooperatively solving problems or, indeed, cooperatively taking examinations.

A last assumption is that individuals go through distinguishable stages of development and that educational techniques and processes must match developmental needs as they arise or the techniques and processes will be relatively fruitless. Nevitt Sanford has handsomely expressed this postulate:[6]

The idea of a "stage" of development rests upon a conception of a course of development, that is to say, an order of events defining progress from lower to higher levels of development. A high level of development in personality is characterized chiefly by complexity and by wholeness. It is expressed in a high degree of differentiation, that is, a large number of different parts having different and specialized functions, and in a high degree of integration, that is, a state of affairs in which communication among parts is great enough so that the different parts may, without losing their essential identity, become organized into larger wholes in order to serve the larger purposes of the person. Using the terms introduced above to stand for the major systems of the personality, we may say that in the highly developed person there is a rich and varied impulse life, many different impulses having now found various modes of expression; conscience has been broadened and refined in the sense that it is sensitive to many different kinds of moral issues; and it is enlightened and individualized; it has been brought under the sway of the ego's processes and so operates in accord with the person's best thought and judgment; the ego's responsiveness to multitudinous aspects of the natural, social, and cultural environment is matched by the diversity of its interrelated sensibilities and adaptive capacities; although it judges events and controls actions in accord with reality, it remains in close enough touch with impulses—the deeper sources of emotion and will—so that there is freedom of imagination and an enduring capacity to be fully alive. This highly developed structure has a fundamental stability which is expressed in consistency of behavior over time; it underlies the individual's sense of direction, his independence of thought and action, and his capacity to make and carry out commitments to others and to himself. But the structure is not fixed once and for all, nor is the consistency of behavior absolute; the highly developed individual is always open to new experience, and capable of further learning; his stability is

---

[6] N. Sanford (Ed.), *The American College* (New York: Wiley, 1962), pp. 257–258.

fundamental in the sense that he can go on developing while remaining essentially himself.

Instructors who would bring a new and revitalized curriculum to their students must change their teaching and advising practices from what is conventional and orthodox. But this is really not asking for something new; rather it is asking that professors practice what great teachers have always practiced. Students recall gratefully, and often with wonder, the traits of great teachers—affection, respect for students' imagination, intellectual freshness, and personal charm.[7]

Helen Keller, talking of her teacher, Ann Mansfield Sullivan, describes their first encounter:

I felt approaching footsteps, I stretched out my hand as I supposed it to be my mother; someone took it and I was caught up close in the arms of her who had come to reveal all things to me and more than all things else, to love me.

John Stuart Mill received most of his education from his father, and describes another technique demanded by new curricula:

From 1810 to the end of 1813 we were living in Newington Green, then an almost rustic neighborhood. My father's health required considerable and constant exercise, and he walked habitually before breakfast, generally in the green lanes toward Hornsey. In these walks, I always accompanied him, and with my earliest recollections of green fields and wild flowers is mingled that of the account I gave him daily of what I had read the day before. To the best of my remembrance this was a voluntary rather than a prescribed exercise.

And James William Crabtree's recollection shows that effective teachers seek to use the idiom of their students:

Miss Moore learned all she could about the animals, birds, and snakes common to that timbered country in order to talk our language better, and in order to tell us more than we knew of the fox,

[7] These vignettes are taken from H. Peterson (Ed.), *Great Teachers* (New York: Vintage, 1946).

the raccoon and the hoot owl. She questioned us and our parents about them. She let us bring our rabbits, raccoons and other pets to school on special occasions.

The genius of Mark Hopkins is revealed in this description of his teaching:

With some qualifications and limitations it may be called a process of rediscovery. It has a remote kinship with the theories of Rousseau and Herbert Spencer who would discard books, set aside history, which records the experience of the past, assume that everything is new, that what is behind us is not worthy of our attention, and attempt to solve the riddle of the universe by retracing anew the experiences of humanity.

Another teacher rejected sterile logic and terminology:

Charles Edward Garman taught a course in logic, not in the formal sense, not the technique of logic, but the practical application of logical methods. In outline his system was simple—the wiping out of preconceived ideas, the search for data, the weighing of evidence, and the groping for conclusions if such were to be found. It is not the conclusions arrived at that remain in the memory, nor yet the material of the course, but the inductive method of reasoning; that, and the peculiar inspiration that must have been largely personal and magnetic.

The power of personality seems frequently of much greater import as is revealed in a description of Francis Barton Gummere:

But what we learned from him lay in the very charm of his personality. It was a spell that no one in his classroom could escape. It shone from his sparkling eye; it spoke in his irresistible humor; it moved in every line of that well-loved face; in his characteristic gesture of leaning forward, and tilting his head a little to one side as he listened patiently to whatever juvenile surmises we stammered to express.

Woodrow Wilson's personality also seems to have left its mark:

So it was that Woodrow Wilson opened the doors of an ampler life to us. As for what he actually taught, it was the inspiration of his personality rather than what he actually taught that caused our hearts to burn within us while he talked with us by the way. His was precisely the type of scholarship which would have won me to the man. Forty years ago this country was swept by the craze for the German type of dry-as-dust scholarship. It was about the time that kiln-dried historical students were toppling Macaulay from his pedestal and enthroning the dreary and meticulous Stubbs in his stead. Let us be thankful that, according to the precepts of the day, Professor Wilson did not undertake an analysis of the function of the Carolingian mayors of the palace or delve into the genealogies of the Hittite kings.

Having students experience life itself rather than book-contained distillates of life seems to have characterized the teaching of Louis Agassiz:

When I sat me down before my tin pan, Agassiz brought me a small fish, placing it before me with the rather stern requirement that I should study it but should on no account talk to anyone concerning it, nor read anything related to fishes until I had his permission to do so. To my inquiry, "What shall I do" he said in effect, "Find out what you can without damaging the specimen. When I think you have done the work I will question you."

It is obvious that the main ingredient of the vivid new experiences students seek is teachers of such outlooks and talent as these memorable ones. Such teachers have always been and will always be the heart of good education.

X

Curriculum Change for Student Needs

It appears that student development requires at least four different sets of educational experiences. The first need is a set of experiences to provide a common universe of discourse—a common body of allusion, illustration, and principle—necessary for people to communicate with each other and to share the same culture. At one level these experiences are provided by television and other mass media, but common learnings at a more sophisticated and richer level are desirable. The general education component of the curriculum should provide this common set of experiences and nothing more. The touchstone as to whether a course should be listed under

150

general education requirements should be: is this course useful to all people living in the last quarter of the twentieth century?

A second component of the curriculum could be called liberal studies, and should consist of courses which students take to broaden their experience and to sample different fields. Liberal studies would be courses in the arts or social sciences taken by the specialist in one of the hard sciences or mathematics.

Then there are those courses essential for a major or concentration, and another group of courses which could be considered contextual. For a history major, courses in political science, economics, or even psychology would be contextual, while for a physics major, courses in mathematics and chemistry would be contextual. While no hard and fast percentages can be posited as a guide (engineers, nurses, and teacher trainees do pose particular problems), general or common education should comprise a fourth, liberal studies a fourth, contextual studies a fourth, and a major a fourth of the student's undergraduate years. To increase the weight of the major beyond a fourth begins to distort the purpose of the undergraduate curriculum and to approximate the mission of advanced professional or graduate education.

Institutions also should give recognition in the curriculum to the concerns of students in their struggles over personal identity and interpersonal relations. Sensitivity training or T-group experience has commanded considerable speculation, enough so that this element might be included in the undergraduate curriculum. One experiment is illustrative. All students in one experimental curriculum take several courses of an orthodox nature but also are divided into small therapy groups which meet once a week under the guidance of an experienced group therapist. These students are also brought into contact with leaders from a variety of fields every two weeks. These adult role models help students test their growing awareness of their own identity. The third phase of this experiment is readings from such authors as Karen Horney, Abraham Maslow, Eric Fromm, and Erik H. Erikson on the theory that reading such writers will help students formulate and answer emerging questions about themselves.

College courses should be organized so that students have

real-life experiences as a counterpoint to the theoretical or academic experiences they have in classrooms. The range of possibilities for such experiences is enormous; several experiments from San Francisco State College are cited as examples. An affective learning project of encounter groups, theater games, body movement, and sensory awareness is an important element of the Creative Development Institute (part of the Experimental College), and it provides degree credit. A crafts, trades, and skills community center provides a way by which disadvantaged youth can learn appropriate skills and college youth can gain academic credit for teaching them. One important project of that center was the training of Negro cameramen who then could use those skills in portraying Negro life from their point of view. A Black Studies Institute is becoming an academic department of the college. Then there is a Community Services Institute in which students couple community work with college credit. The program trains community organizers and stresses attacks on such problems as frustration, the need for creative expression, isolation from neighbors, and a sense of political powerlessness.

A matter which frequently is not faced realistically is what courses or experiences are really defensible in terms of the purposes of an educational program. If one assumes that the purpose of the general education component of the undergraduate curriculum is to provide that common body of knowledge, insight, principle, allusion, and illustration needed by everyone to cope with reality and to communicate effectively with others, then one may question the inclusion of some courses and exclusion of others. For example, in the late 1960s which is more important for this common learning purpose—a course in natural science or a course including law, economics, and the realities of a postindustrial society? We could argue that since science plays such a crucial role in contemporary life, no person should be without an awareness of the basic modes of thought and presuppositions of science. But if we judge by the actual problems most people experience, the actual subjects of conversation of all but scientists and their interpreters, we could argue that science as such does not really play a central role in the common experiences and discourses of most people. This is not to argue that science has no place in the undergraduate curriculum, nor even that science should not be included in the educational experiences of most people. Indeed, the counterargument is compelling. But it is just possible that courses in science should be classified under some other curriculum rubric than general education.

To etch this issue more clearly, consider two possible sets of general education requirements:

First, traditional general education requirements (most often taken during the first two years but sometimes spread over four years) usually form a program roughly equivalent to one-fourth of the requirements for a baccalaureate degree. The program could consist of a course in the humanities which stresses the Western tradition and probes selected artistic, architectural, philosophic, and literary expressions of various ages; a course in social science which interrelates materials from sociology, anthropology, psychology, economics, and political science; a course in natural science which either interrelates materials from both the physical and the biological sciences or stresses one or the other; and a course in communications which develops skills of writing and speaking. Such a curriculum at least samples the broad domains of human knowledge and is defensible in the light of orthodox traditions of the liberal arts and sciences. However, this program may be vulnerable to the charge that it still does not consider the concerns which commonly perplex college students and the entire adult population of the nation.

Second, another conception of general education also consists of approximately one-fourth of the requirements for a baccalaureate degree and is spread throughout the four undergraduate years. A course on ethics and theology expressed in the contemporary idiom raises and discusses questions like these: What is the proper stance for a conscientious objector? What are the theological implications of heart transplants? What are the ethical and theological presuppositions of the growing need for law and order? Another course involves law, economics, and the organizational and structural conditions of a postindustrial society that is rapidly becoming urbanized. This course seeks to help students understand themselves in relationship to an increasingly complex society. A course in literature presents students with a wide range of literary materials, some in contemporary idioms, to evoke aesthetic and emotional response. The aim is to avoid extensive analysis and to expose students to many literary works, with a primary purpose of helping them expand their impulse lives. A one-semester course in writing and an elective course chosen from a limited pool of courses created to meet general education needs completes a student's program.

There are also questions about other parts of the undergraduate curriculum. There is a tendency to offer specialized courses at the upper division on the grounds that students need such specialization to prepare for graduate school or that a valid major must contain a high degree of specialization. We know, however, that the majority of undergraduate students do not enter careers related to their undergraduate majors, and that slightly less than half the students who attend graduate school do not concentrate on subjects in which they majored or concentrated as undergraduate students. And in view of the rapidly changing labor market, it seems likely that most who receive a bachelor's degree will shift their callings two, three, or four times during a lifetime. If the actual needs and desires of students for specialization were considered, offerings listed in college catalogs could be critically reduced, which might also solve the problem of the institution which offers more specialized courses than its faculty resources will allow.

Coupled with this point is the frequently made observation that the utilization of leisure will become a more important concern in the lives of most American adults than will a vocation. The phenomenon is already observable in the lives of middle-class women who find that household appliances save much time that would ordinarily be spent on household tasks. The same condition may quickly be faced by all, for leisure may be the most important factor for the next generation: 2 per cent of the population will be able to produce all the goods and food that the other 98 per cent consume. Leisure will replace work as man's most time-consuming activity. At a 1964 meeting of leading political and social scientists, the president of the American Academy of Political and Social Science recommended such revolutionary measures as the establishment of departments of leisure in the fifty states and the compulsory teaching of leisure skills in the public schools. He was immediately challenged from the floor as hopelessly conservative in his approach. An economist at the meeting claimed that "we face such an explosive increase in leisure that within a mere ten years we may have to keep the unemployed portion of our population under sedation unless we can quickly figure out something better for them to do."[1]

It would seem that much more attention to skills and appreciation for leisure should be given in the undergraduate curriculum than is now given. This calls for enjoyment of literature (rather than distaste for reading), satisfaction in sports, and especially skill and pleasure in conversation. Perhaps the following question might be used in serious curriculum study: Assuming that, regardless of calling, most graduates of the undergraduate college are going to experience long stretches of leisure time, not only during their productive years but in years of retirement as well, What experiences should they be given to ensure that this leisure can be managed and can produce fuller human development? At the moment it seems unlikely that this issue will be resolved, but there are forces in operation which may bring about a change. Several projects of the National Foundation for the Humanities have demonstrated that talented students are severely penalized by existing admissions and curriculum structures. Studies of creative students have underscored the same point. As evidence mounts, faculties may be willing to modify previously held positions.

We know enough of student needs, desires, and demands to point to directions in which curriculum structure should move. However, such radical modifications of existing practice generate a number of issues which must be faced before radical curriculum revision can take place.

First, there is concern that although students are asking for such revision of the curriculum, they really do not want it and would not patronize an institution which departed too drastically from orthodox patterns. Liberal arts colleges fear that unless they offer courses clearly parallel to those offered by major graduate institutions, students simply will not attend, feeling that for such high tuition they should be assured of the transferability of credits. There is

[1] E. W. Gordon, "The Culturally Different, Deprived, or Economically Marginal Student: A Challenge to Education," in L. B. Mayhew (Ed.), *Higher Education in the Revolutionary Decades* (Berkeley, Calif.: McCutchan, 1968), p. 380.

at present insufficient evidence to indicate whether this fear is warranted, but the experiences of two different institutions suggest that it is not.

The freshman-year program at Antioch College represents a radical departure through such things as freeing students from attending classes and providing a number of courses organized simply by asking interested people to sign up on a bulletin board. The program encountered some faculty resistance, but it apparently met with great student enthusiasm. While eventually the program at Antioch may represent a blend of orthodox procedures and some of the new styles, responsible officials believe that the college will never go back completely to the old style of curriculum offering. At San Francisco State College, the free university sort of course was assimilated by the institution itself. Its experimental college quickly attained and has maintained the optimum size of about 2,400 registrants.

Even more vexing is the question as to whether faculty members trained in graduate school can adapt to new curriculum approaches. Faculty members form their ideas as to what is proper in the curriculum through exposure to graduate sequences of courses, which focus on the systematic development of knowledge, and they may not be able to conceive of any other way of organizing knowledge and experience. They find the techniques of instruction—lecturing, instructor-led discussion groups, seminar work, and the preparation of papers—compatible and cannot conceive that students can learn in other ways. There is other evidence to suggest that many students are, in fact, creating an underground curriculum which makes sense to them but which would horrify their graduate school trained professors. Whether this underground curriculum can be legitimatized must depend on whether faculty members can adjust to it.

A serious question is raised as to whether major curriculum innovation can take place in the large, complex institutions in which most students will receive their undergraduate education. In dealing with large numbers, the argument runs, modular curriculum units and categorical requirements are mandatory if chaos is to be avoided. According to this viewpoint, it is possible for small institutions like Goddard College, Marlboro College, or even Antioch

College to experiment because their student populations are limited, but Michigan State University, University of Illinois, and University of California, with their forty to eighty thousand students, cannot experiment and therefore must adopt standardized procedures.

It can be argued, however, that the basic unit for manipulation is the faculty-student ratio, and that this ratio can allow great flexibility which can be organized by computerized course accounting. For example, a faculty member's load in a complex institution is divided into three portions. One-third of his time is devoted to a graduate seminar, another third to an upper-level orthodox course, and during the final third of his time he is available to develop whatever sort of ad hoc course he and a number of self-selected students decide upon. The expectation is that the student also devotes perhaps a third of his time to ad hoc educational activity.

The matter of quality control is also important. Traditionally, quality control over courses has been maintained by the fact that faculty groups actually approved new curriculum ventures. In a complex institution such as the University of California, this may require nine to twelve months. However, quality control could be decentralized and the process speeded up. Perhaps within each major subunit of a school or college a quality control agency could be created with the power to act quickly on requests for new courses. This does require trust, but, after all, the entire profession of education is predicated on an assumed trust and faith.

A related issue is whether some of these new curriculum ideas can be applied to professional schools. Professional schools, governed as they are by the professions they serve, believe they have an obligation to ensure that each student follows a sequential arrangement of courses to ensure minimum competency. An engineer, so the argument runs, must have a full complement of basic science courses and must have had enough laboratory and field work so that when he builds a bridge or designs a highway it will work. Such a belief must accommodate several disquieting observations. Christopher Jencks and David Riesman observe that as the faculties of professional schools become more professional in their orientation they are inclined to pay less attention to the demands of practitioners in the field. The professors themselves decide what the students should study, and the profession accepts those who are screened through this process. Thus, if professors within professional schools wish to do so, they can change distinctly the pattern of experiences required of their students, in the full expectation that graduates would remain certifiable.

A few professional schools have begun seriously to change curriculum patterns and apparently have run into no great obstacles. The Yale Medical School, for example, has arranged for first-year medical students to have clinical experience as one means of showing the young medical student what illness is like, and at the same time meeting the needs of these young students for altruistic expression. The Princeton University School of Architecture is placing first-year students in work situations in urban conditions rather than concentrating on theoretical or exclusively academic modes of training.

A parallel issue is the possible adverse reactions of important constituencies to the institution. If a college changes radically its concept of general education, will the regional accrediting agencies approve it? Would a regional accrediting agency, for example, be willing to accredit an institution that was strong in the arts but that did not require a balanced spread of academically oriented courses? Even more serious, in view of state certification and licensing requirements, is the question as to whether an institution can depart too far from established norms and still have its graduates certified. In California, for example, forty-five hours of general education are required for teacher certification, and those courses must be of a certain prescribed sort. If a state college departed from this pattern, there is some question that its graduates could obtain their teaching credentials.

Then, too, there is what graduate schools require in the way of prior training on the part of applicants. There is the fear that graduate schools would reject students whose transcripts revealed a number of ad hoc problem-centered courses in place of the readily recognized sequences of courses labeled in traditional ways. And, of course, parents educated in other times have expectations which might be at variance with what an innovative institution was attempting. For example, the private liberal arts college which depends on tuition charges sees itself as particularly vulnerable in this respect.

Once again, however, there is insufficient evidence upon which to generalize.

Enough examples of successful deviation from norms indicate that modification is possible. Stephens College has for over forty years offered a number of atypical courses designed especially with the needs of women in mind, and has experienced very little difficulty in transferring its students to other institutions or in maintaining accreditation. It recently shifted from a two-year to a four-year institution offering a unique sort of bachelor's program, and received high praise at the time of accreditation for daring to break with tradition. Antioch and Sarah Lawrence have long been experimental and continue to attract students of high ability who appear for the most part to be acceptable to graduate and professional schools once they have been certified by the college. What seems to be necessary is for the college to establish standards of excellence in the light of its own perceived mission, and then to communicate its techniques to important constituencies in understandable ways. Thus, the institution which sends a high proportion of its students on to graduate school must explain to receiving graduate institutions what it is doing and why.

The educational needs of highly talented students in the arts is a serious issue. Students in the arts with professional aspirations seem to require a steeping in the medium in which their talents lie, and they may very well have deficiencies in domains considered important by verbally or numerically oriented faculty members. Two questions arise: Will college admissions committees, which are for the most part faculty-dominated, admit the highly talented student with academic deficiencies? And will the faculty tolerate a curriculum which is tailored to the needs of some talented students?

A bachelor's degree must stand for something, the argument runs, and one cannot really quarrel with this. But should it in every case stand for the same thing? The Negro institution that requires two years of a foreign language might serve its students better by developing competence in English and by helping Negro students deal with the paranoia which comes from minority caste status. The small women's Roman Catholic college serving a second-generation ethnic constituency from Central Europe should have a curriculum which is substantively different from that offered by an Eastern men's college attracting for the most part fifth- or sixth-generation college-educated clientele.

Throughout this book the argument has been advanced that fundamental needs and urges of undergraduate students should be accommodated in the curriculum. An issue arises from the professional feelings of faculty members who believe that they know what is good for students and that the decision about the curriculum should ultimately be made in terms of criteria established by the faculty. This point of view is poignantly expressed by the faculty member who remarked in all seriousness that "to base a curriculum on the needs of students is obscene." We agree that ultimate decisions about the curriculum should be professional and should be made by the faculty, but this does not obviate the need to understand as fully and deeply as possible what the development of late-adolescent students requires in experience and training. Perhaps the only argument which can be advanced is that students do not seem to gain appreciably from the curriculum efforts established by professors. If those efforts, which cost 60 to 70 per cent of an institution's operating budget, are to be effective, some changes should be made—and change in the direction suggested by students might result in greater effectiveness.

A final issue, closely related to the previous one, involves the needs of faculty and the needs of students, and the question of which needs should be satisfied if they conflict with each other. Students say they need leisure, and they need some intimate contact with at least *a* professor. They need materials which make psychological sense to them, and they need freedom to make many decisions for themselves. These needs frequently conflict with basic needs of faculty members. It is likely that the faculty member who has studied a subject intensively needs to communicate it in his own way to others. He may require for his own development an audience to whom he can talk about what concerns him. It is also possible that the faculty member, because of the kind of person he is, wants some kind of master-disciple relationship with students. Because the faculty member gains his greatest security from rationality, he might feel uncomfortable dealing with materials having a heavy emotional load.

This point can be illustrated by one institution which freed students to attend or not attend professorial presentations, as the students chose. The students enjoyed this freedom, stayed away from presentations, and seemingly made as great gains as had students from previous years who had rigidly and rigorously attended classes. However, the professors whose presentations were unattended suffered severe feelings of threat, anxiety, and great disappointment. Probably these conflicting needs must always remain in tension, but it is possible to argue that in event of direct confrontation, the needs of the student should prevail. Education is still a helping profession with a mission of facilitating human development. This point of view may and probably should require a sublimation of some feelings by professors.

The actual construction of a curriculum requires the resolution of many troublesome issues, and while no one undergraduate curriculum can work for all institutions, nevertheless the elements of a model curriculum can be presented. At least four kinds of study ought properly to be found in the educational experience of all students, although the proportion of time devoted to any one kind should be negotiable. These are the previously cited general, basic, or common studies; liberal or broadening studies; contextual studies; and studies of some depth reflected in a field of concentration or a major. In spite of powerful cultural forces pressing for the distinct development of individuals, college students should acquire in common certain skills, knowledge, and ideals, some appropriate common learnings. But students also need to explore new subjects and to feed curiosity, even if it be a dilettante sort of curiosity. They should almost be forced to elect experiences different from those in which they specialize. These experiences are here labeled as liberal or broadening studies. Probably most students benefit from some concentrated work in a limited area if only for the sake of seeing just how complex a single field is. Thus, the major or concentration is supportable. But that concentration is meaningful only if it is done in an appropriate context. Hence, contextual studies are suggested.

Another curriculum element is strongly suggested by the

demands and criticisms undergraduate students have advanced. They sense that they need varied experiences if they are to develop in a comprehensive way. Several are listed, but this list is not necessarily exhaustive.

(1) Every student should have the opportunity to engage in independent study in which he sets his own goals, proceeds at his own rate, decides when he has finished, and feels free to use or not use professorial resources the institution provides. This independent work should not be confused with a scheduled tutorial arrangement, where the volition seems to rest with the professor. Rather, it should be an opportunity for students to succeed or fail on their own.

(2) Every student should learn in large and impersonal situations. As adults, much learning comes either through mass media or in large group lectures and the like, and college students should be able to do this without feeling threatened or lonely. At least one large lecture course might be part of the experience of every student, with no discussion groups, laboratory groups, or further assistance provided.

(3) Students also need to learn to function in small groups, and they need the encouragement which a small group develops. The curriculum should be structured so that every student has a sustained experience in a small group, and the time should be long enough so that the group could take on many of the characteristics of a primary group.

(4) Every student should have a relationship with an adult professional person which is sustained over a long enough period of time so that the adult can serve as an appropriate role model, parent surrogate, and friend with whom the student can test his emerging notions of reality. This relationship is probably the most important single experience students require.

(5) Every student should have a sustained off-campus experience of some sort. Whether this is cooperative work-study, an overseas experience, or the opportunity simply to study on one's own in a distant city is less important than that the student is encouraged to look beyond the campus walls.

(6) Every student should have the opportunity to know intimately a culture or subculture different from his own. This may come from studying in a foreign university, from doing cadet teach-

ing in a culture substantially different from the student's own, or from serving as a participant-observer, infiltrating a subculture distinctly different.

(7) Every student should be required to make a sustained effort over a prolonged period of time on some task. There should be some courses, possibly quite a few, that extend over a full year or more, with final assessment left until the very end. The traits to be developed here are not unlike those generated by work on a doctoral thesis.

(8) Every student should have opportunities to engage in a number of brief ad hoc activities, which should have the same curriculum value as longer efforts. Students should be encouraged to experiment and explore, but should not be expected to make major time commitments to such activities. It is conceivable that a number of explorations might consume no more than a week or two each.

(9) Every student should enjoy, unpenalized, opportunities to engage in play for his personal satisfaction.

(10) Every student should have opportunities to gain deeper understanding of his own emotions and those of others. Sensitivity training, group therapy, individual counseling, and similar activities can lead to this understanding.

(11) Every student should have a chance to learn by using the new media. Society is reaching the point where every college student should learn something with the aid of a computer and with a programed course using audiovisual aids, direct observation, and reading. The new media are so important that college graduates might be considered illiterate if they have not learned to use them.

(12) Every student should have an aesthetically creative experience, regardless of the level of his performance. This suggests some form of required studio work just for the satisfaction of creating.

These experiences should result in certain student competencies which are an obligation of education. The following skills are desired and needed by students, demanded by the society into which they will move, and of legitimate concern to college teachers. College graduates should be able: (1) to read, write, speak, and listen with some sophistication in subjects of concern to people living in the

last half of the twentieth century; (2) to recognize personal problems and issues and to be able to resolve them with the best possible
information and assistance; (3) to know and use a library and
other bibliographic aids—printed matter and other media; (4) to
cooperate intimately with others in solving complex problems; (5)
to distinguish between cognition and affection and to be able to
use both rationality and feeling for satisfaction of the total person;
(6) to relate in both evaluative and nonevaluative ways to other
people, and to understand the appropriateness of each; (7) to enjoy
one's own activities without threat or guilt if those activities are unusual and not commonly valued by others; (8) to identify gaps in
one's own experience or learning, and to find ways to fill them;
(9) to understand computers and other ways of arriving at quantitative knowledge, and to recognize both the capabilities and limitations of quantification; (10) to know and express one's own values
and to defend them and modify them when the occasion requires.

The fourth and final element of a model curriculum is
probably dearer to the academicians' hearts than the three previously elaborated. This element has two major components. The
first involves the major divisions of human knowledge which come
into existence and subdivide following the lead of research and
inquiry. The subjects listed in a curriculum will be determined by
the mission of an institution, by the training and experience of its
faculty members, and by the needs of the clientele to be served.
However, all students should be exposed to some knowledge of the
Western European tradition, American civilization, at least one non-
Western civilization, the broad domain of science, and some technology and mathematics. And they should do some interdisciplinary
work which can suggest how various subjects illuminate each other.

The second component consists of the several ways of knowing, ranging from the starkest sort of empiricism at one extreme to
intuition and revealed truth at the other. Since all humans must
make use of these different ways of perceiving reality, the college
curriculum should at least sensitize students to the attributes, capabilities, and limitations of each. With the demands college students
currently are making, overemphasizing the descriptive, the phenom-
enological, and the intuitive is probably wise. Such emphasis would
come through courses in philosophy, the arts, and theology. Con-

cepts of empiricism, experimentation, and statistical manipulation could be contained in courses in the natural sciences or behavioral sciences. Mathematics can be taught empirically, descriptively, or even aesthetically.

This four-part model is eclectic and is not intended for exact duplication at any institution. Rather, it suggests a way of thinking about curricula in times of enormous social change. Its purpose, as is that of the entire book, is to declare that the contemporary college student needs and can have a contemporary curriculum.

XI

Toward a
Theory of
Curriculum

As we approach the end of this book, it seems appropriate to review some of the major points with a view to sketching the broad outlines of a theory of curriculum. Any theory must be based upon postulates. Once created, the theory should then produce hypotheses for testing and, ultimately, the elaboration of still further postulates. A theory of undergraduate curriculum rests on several postulates.

The first is the student's need for structure—structure within which his life is organized and structure for whatever he is dealing with. Jerome Bruner says that once the structure of a subject is exposed, an individual can then acquire details throughout his life with which to elaborate that structure. Undergraduate students

166

need to apprehend not only the structure of a subject but the structure within which the curriculum, the extracurriculum, and their personal lives are organized.

The second postulate is that every human being is searching for significance, for reason, for meaning. Experiments on how children learn suggest that if meaning can be assigned to things, learning takes place much more rapidly than if things are organized in a random or nonsense pattern. Undergraduate students today, particularly that minority out of whose activities will come the dimensions of the curriculum of the future, repeatedly use the words *significance* and *relevance* as they criticize the existing college structure. The humanities and the social sciences have failed to respond to this desire of undergraduate students for relevance and significance. Very likely the sciences have been equally culpable, but scientists have been able to persuade students otherwise.

Rose Goldsen of Cornell points out that because of the present intellectual climate, students are willing to put up with considerable drudgery and not a little nonsense in science classes because scientists have convinced them that drudgery and nonsense are necessary for something the students ultimately want. This is pseudorelevance which students have been talked into accepting. She argues that people in the social sciences and humanities have not been similarly successful. Students come to courses in psychology really wanting insights into their own emotions and motivations, but they are introduced to the physiology of perception. Students come to the humanities wanting some contact with the ideas of grief and joy, death and life, and instead they get scholarly textual criticism and memorization of names and terms. Much of the criticism leveled at these subjects stems from their lack of significance, and one of the reasons the free university idea has caught hold is because it purports to assign relevance to what is being read and discussed.

The third postulate, of a somewhat different order from the first two, is that good educational practice is likely to be good business and good management practice. The idea that the college or university is not a business and is conducted by other standards and methods has long been abroad. There is something to commend this point of view: an institution may offer a number of esoteric courses for which there is no immediate demand or return on educational grounds. But the institution should make its decision to offer little-used material on rational grounds and not just because of capricious interest. One needs to look at how efficient the curriculum is, how well each of the courses draws students, how well each measures against the rest, and how much each course costs. Especially in the undergraduate curriculum, when one finds a course which is uneconomical because it has attracted few students over a long period of time, one is likely to have found a course which is not much good anyway.

The fourth postulate is that any system of education should have a built-in process for bringing about regular change. Some have argued that the entire curriculum should be revised every five years. While such an automatic arrangement might be a trifle extreme, procedures should be such that change is expected and is not associated only with the inauguration of a new administration or a major palace revolt.

The fifth postulate is that the purpose of the curriculum is to change people and to move people in desirable directions. This implies that education is a rational activity and that professional educators can, by looking at the expressed needs of their clients and the expressed and implied needs of society, determine what sorts of people society wants and needs. The curriculum is, or should be, one of the important devices by which this comes about. Some may label this indoctrination, but one need not be afraid of indoctrination if by that term is meant the attempt, by a variety of means, to move people from one point to another, and the ability to describe in advance where they are going.

The sixth postulate is that every part of the educational effort of an institution should be consistent with every other part. The colleges which Phillip Jacob, George Stern, C. Robert Pace, and Paul Heist describe as having a peculiar potency to make changes in people seem to have a number of things in common, one of which is that the whole institution, including its curriculum, reflects the interrelationships of a consistent philosophic point of view. In contrast, a college which emphasizes intellectual freedom and seeks to encourage students to do independent intellectual work but also maintains a rigid custodial relationship to students is likely to be ineffective both intellectually and custodially.

The seventh postulate is that the principle of parsimony should apply to the curriculum just as much as it applies to research. What is the simplest explanation to account for all of the variables? In curriculum terms, what is the simplest organization, the fewest number of courses which can bring about, or have a reasonable chance of bringing about, the change in students in which the college is interested? Overelaboration of curricula is no particular virtue, much as it might please the specialized tendencies of individual faculty members.

Eighth is the postulate that the late-adolescent period in the life of Americans is a unique and distinct period within which individuals manifest several discrete needs. The late-adolescent student is in need of new kinds of relationships with people. He is seeking to break away from reliance on parents as primary role models, but he is really seeking, in a good sense of the word, a parent surrogate. Hence, he does need some kinds of personal relationships with adults in this new professional capacity. He is also in need of new kinds of group relationships. Currently, for example, students seek membership in relatively small groups in which they can interrelate at an intimate level.

The ninth and final postulate is that each level of education should be articulated with other levels and with life outside of the curriculum. This does not mean that each level is exclusively preparing students for the next level. One can be critical of the high school which adjusts its curriculum to the demands of the college, the undergraduate college that tailors its program to the graduate school, and the junior college that adjusts its program to the four-year school. Such institutions have forsaken their essential selves. Rather, articulation should be close but the ordering of relationships should be reversed. As the elementary school identifies the needs of the preelementary and elementary school children and develops a program to meet those needs, the secondary school should take cognizance of that program and make its adjustment accordingly. The college should relate downward to the various styles which the secondary schools have produced rather than forcing the secondary schools to relate upward. Obviously this cannot be completely a one-way effort, but the emphasis should be to build upward rather than to impose downward.

With these postulates in mind, each institution can work toward the development of its own curriculum stance. In so doing, however, certain essential procedures must be kept in mind.

First is the need for honest concern by an institution for what it wants to do to its students. Unfortunately, there is considerable copying in higher education. The phenomenon of most institutions throughout the country looking yearningly at the selective few as models is inappropriate for a pluralistic society. The nation can tolerate only a limited number of Harvards. Sometimes one could wish that John Gardner has never coined the term *excellence* because institution after institution is now trying for excellence defined in extremely limited and restricted ways.

There is enormous variation among institutions of higher education in this country—a variation which should be, but is not, reflected in curriculum and teaching. In one institution awarding the A.B. degree, the median student ranked in the top 5 per cent of high school graduates and the top 5 per cent of those taking the Scholastic Aptitude Tests, while in another institution, the median student ranked in the bottom 20 per cent on both high school rank and academic aptitude. There are degree-granting institutions which still provide the acculturation function of moving first and second generation children of foreign-born families into the mainstream of American middle-class life, while other institutions, awarding the same degrees, make the assumption that students have already acquired basic American values before college. Honesty requires that each college assess its own reality and accept it before stating its educational goals.

Second, the college should make an attempt to discover the ritualistic or nonfunctioning parts of its curriculum. Nonfunctioning parts are those which a candid, realistic appraisal would suggest have little chance of bringing about the desired changes in students. For example, one or two years of studying a foreign language will not give students much sensitivity into the foreign culture (one can imagine how French students would judge American culture based upon simplistic interpretations of America found in a textbook) or develop facility in speaking and reading the language. All course requirements should be examined. Those that do not produce the desired results should be discarded or made more effective. In the case of foreign language, for example, a reasonable alternative is to insist that students take enough foreign language to develop a reasonable facility in it.

Third, the institution should subject the entire curriculum to constant criticism and analysis. While the entire faculty cannot make continuous self-studies, since self-study inquiry is an extremely tiring activity, the newly forming offices of institutional research provide a device for appropriate continual analysis of the curriculum. In this context, institutional research can be defined as the continuing internal audit of the educational program of the institution.

Fourth, since education is basically a way by which important elements of a culture are passed on to new generations, the colleges need to develop ways of accumulating evidence about what society needs to have transmitted to youth and what can, in fact, be transmitted. Other social institutions are also involved in this process, but in a complex, developed society the education system must be involved. Too often the curriculum has been constructed without particular reference to such matters, obeying instead a tradition or a myth.

Perhaps the point can be illustrated by considering the content of courses in general education, that portion of formal education which is concerned with preparing students for their non-vocational roles as citizen, family member, leisure-enjoying individual, and problem solver. It is the education which provides the common universe of discourse people need in order to communicate with each other. Content could be derived from absolute postulates, as was medieval scholasticism, but this results in an education which ultimately loses meaning for students. A more effective content can be derived by studying the way people live and then developing methods for preparing students to similarly engage themselves.

A college should accumulate evidence over a period of years about what its graduates are doing, what parts of the curriculum they say helped them most, and what changes in the curriculum they believe would be appropriate. Further, the college should maintain close contact with its supporting public in order to ascertain the public's wants and needs. If there is a clear increase in the desire or need for proficiency in a foreign language or for greater awareness of non-Western cultures, then the content of the curriculum should be modified. The liberal arts college which asks the future employers of its graduates what they expect of college educated men and women is similarly illustrating the technique. Such a process is time-consuming and many colleges are attempting to bypass it, but if one wishes to develop a rational curriculum there is no substitute for it.

Some may object to this approach on grounds that the college ought to lead rather than follow, but such an objection overlooks the fact that basically the college is a norming institution. It is not intended to create people who reject the prevailing cultural values. Rather, it prepares people to enter the mainstream of life in that society. Presently, for example, a major problem is the education of the culturally deprived. An education which drives Negro youth further from the central tendencies of American middle-class society does neither youth nor society good. Rather, the college should identify the important knowledge, skills, and attitudes which enable people to survive in the American context and make these the substance of the curriculum. Another example is the inclusion of Negro history into the general education of most students so that a more acceptable climate is established for full entry, on terms of equality, of the American Negro into the mainstream of American life.

The substance of the curriculum should be those elements of culture which have the highest survival value for a particular clientele at a particular point in time. The institution, through careful scholarship and research, must make an effort to identify changes in the society and to identify contemporary survival values. For instance, the great need may be to train people for the utilization of leisure. It is possible that the current emphasis on specialized vocational training in junior colleges is thirty or forty years too late. One can argue that if it were not for the present war in Viet Nam and the associated defense build-up, the full impact of a growingly cybernated society would be felt through mass unemployment. One can anticipate the time when even some professional roles will be fulfilled by automated services. It is possible also to speculate that in the foreseeable future, well within the lifetime of middle-aged adults, 10 or 20 per cent of the total population will be able to man the entire productive enterprise. Tying personal identity to personal calling will be no longer feasible.

Other cultural changes which the college must identify and adjust to in curricular or extracurricular terms relate to traditional value systems. What kinds of value statements shall institutions present to young people? The curriculum must accommodate itself to problems caused by rapid and fundamental shifts in society, and since some cultural elements become obsolete so quickly, continuous research is necessary. As one example, young people need help in developing personal value stances on things such as sexual behavior in the light of the revolutionary development of the pill.

Last, the curriculum of the college should be genuinely related to pedagogical realities. A student course load at many institutions is five different subjects taken at the same time, but anyone who expects students to study five different subjects is in for a disappointment. Catalogs typically state that students are expected to study two hours outside of class for every hour in class, and in many institutions this also opens areas for disillusionment. In theory college teaching and college subjects are different from high school work because colleges emphasize generalization and they presuppose possession of the relevant corpus of facts, but these claims should be tested by reality. Unduly heavy faculty teaching loads invite the most superficial sort of two-textbook teaching in which the poorer textbook is assigned to the students and the lectures are based on the better one. Only by limiting the number of separate preparations can there be any hope that the college teacher will be able to keep up with the material available.

With similar reasoning, one can argue that no student shall be allowed to take more than three courses at any one time, and preferably no more than four different courses over a full year. One can also argue that with the exception of only a few courses, no more than one and one-half hours of formal face-to-face classroom contact should be permitted during any given week for a course. It is demanding more than human ability allows to expect a professor to be truly creative in a fifteen-week semester course that meets three times a week. Relevant here is Benjamin Bloom's description of "peak learning experiences" (cited earlier), during which the energies of the organism are so focused on the object that months and even years later the individual can register total recall. By limiting classroom contact, it might be possible for faculty members to contrive more of these peak learning experiences.

In light of these elements essential to curriculum construction and the postulates outlined earlier, we suggest several limiting dimensions useful in working toward a general theory of curriculum. One dimension is a philosophy of education. The point has been made already that those colleges which have had a marked impact on the lives of students are those which operate from a consistent philosophic position which pervades the entire institution. It does not seem to make much difference what the philosophy is. A St. John's College can operate from what Harold Taylor would call a rationalistic position and change its students as much as does a Goddard College, which emphasizes pure instrumentalism.

Clearly, however, the prevailing philosophy of education of an institution will make some difference in the content of the curriculum. Three current philosophies of general education have been identified by Harold Taylor. Rationalists base the curriculum on eternal truths and stress the great documents which have survived in civilization. Instrumentalists believe that goals and objectives are constantly changing and that materials should change as individual needs change. Neo-Humanists are more eclectic, using material of traditional value modified in accordance with changing idioms. A rationalist would teach Thomas Aquinas as reflecting eternal verities, the Neo-Humanist might teach him to illustrate the intellectual development of Western civilization, and the instrumentalist would teach him only if an individual student discovered a personal need for knowledge about St. Thomas.

The important point is that the writings of St. Thomas need to be treated as cultural elements with relevance for students of today's generation. If this is not the case, and the adherents to a specific philosophy still insist upon teaching him, students will gradually reject the institution emphasizing an archaic curriculum. The fact that colleges subscribing to the Yale Report of 1828 gradually lost viability, the fact that during the 1930s and 1940s language enrollments declined, and the fact that students in Roman Catholic colleges are currently forcing revision of theology courses illustrates this point.

Viewed in this light, a philosophy of education is as likely to determine pedagogy as curriculum content. The concept of revolution is taught one way if one believes that there are a limited number of basic ideas in Western civilization, the understanding of which should constitute the purpose of education. It is taught another way if one's purpose is to understand the development of twentieth century man. And it is taught in another way if a student is trying to discover how conflicts such as those in which he personally may be engaged actually are resolved. But the concept of revolution is taught in all three systems.

A chart can be a useful technique for conceptualizing a curriculum. One dimension on the chart should be the subject areas to be included in the curriculum, and the other dimension on the chart should include the skills, traits, and attitudes necessary to use the substantive materials well. Benjamin S. Bloom's *Taxonomy of Education Objectives: The Cognitive Domain,* and David Krathwohl's *The Affective Domain* suggest some of the things which could be included on the vertical axis of this chart: observation, classification, and measurement; analysis and synthesis; questions and answers; objectivity; skepticism; evaluation; interpretation; evidence; historical method; geographical approach; causation; dignity of man; empathy; loyalty; freedom and equality. If the collegiate curriculum can be visualized as this two-way chart, with the divisions of knowledge extending along the horizontal axis and the skills, traits, approaches, and attitudes along the vertical axis, then it is possible to plot the important curriculum matters which should be offered and to expose imbalances and omissions.

This chart may be viewed as the first step in thinking about a college-wide curriculum, the offerings of a division or department, or even the construction of a single course. The framework provides the limits within which courses can be built, added, and subtracted. This idea is not unlike the idea that a work of art results when the energy of the artist experiences the limitation of the medium. The chart provides a curricular medium which imposes quite definite, stringent limitations within which the creative energies of the faculty must operate. The faculty should always have the right to put anything it wants into the curriculum, but within sufficient limitations so that the creative act results in curriculum artistry.

Another variety of limitations is illustrated by some general principles of curriculum construction stated by Paul L. Dressel:

(1) All curriculums should start with a 25 per cent institution-wide core or general education requirement. It is not necessary that the core be defined by a few courses required of all students, but it is necessary that the courses be planned for breadth and be equally suitable for all students.

(2) All curriculums should require an additional 30 per cent of the initial 120 credit hours in courses generally accepted as included in the liberal arts and sciences, although these courses may not always be located in the college of arts and sciences.

(3) All curriculums in a single vocational college should include a common group of courses adding up to at least 10 per cent of the total requirement.

(4) Each major or curriculum should also specify a common depth or specialization requirement of 15 per cent of the degree requirement, or approximately three-fifths of the credit requirements for a department major.

(5) Approximately 10 per cent of the initial 120 credit hours should be reserved for an elective major component or for specialization directed toward subvocations in the general field for which a college curriculum is regarded as preparatory.

(6) All curriculums should leave uncommitted at least twelve credits (10 per cent) for electives to be chosen by the student and his adviser.

(7) All curriculums should be carefully screened to insure that the goals are reasonably attainable in a four-year program (or other specified period) and that the courses and other educational experiences required for this attainment are appropriate in the college or university.

(8) Any credit course should either develop or utilize a definable substantive body of content. Skills of a repetitive, how-to-do-it nature should be minimized as course objectives and relegated to the laboratory, to field experience, or simply specified as required demonstrable levels of competency for acceptance, continuance, or graduation in the field.

(9) Each department should offer only one major (although there must be obvious exceptions, as in foreign languages). A few

courses at the junior or senior year may be oriented to subspecialties, but otherwise specialization should be at the postgraduate level.

(10) Department specialization beyond the common requirement should be in courses offered at the junior and senior levels and developed on the assumption that the common requirements are either prerequisites or taken concurrently.

(11) Special courses or sections for majors in other fields should be resisted, unless the need for them can be demonstrated to be more fundamental than a matter of one or two credits or a slightly different selection or organization of content materials.

(12) Introductory course offerings in the basic arts and sciences should be developed in relation to the needs of the total college or university rather than on narrow, specialized department concerns. Only thus is it possible to insist that each technical or professional curriculum use these basic courses in preference to developing its own.

(13) With possibly a few exceptions, courses should be planned on a four- or five-credit basis, with the exception that class sessions, especially in courses beyond the freshman year, may be less than the number of credits.[1]

(14) Laboratory requirements in all courses should be reduced to a minimum by carefully defining the objectives and by providing the means whereby student achievement of these objectives can be determined.

(15) Departments in areas attractive as general electives may appropriately offer an advanced course or two at the junior or senior level without prerequisites other than the relevant courses of the general core requirement. Since these courses would not fall into the sequential course organization of the departments it is probable that they would not be counted as satisfying the major requirements of the departments. The presence of such electives would permit and encourage students to broaden the scope of their

---

[1] If the four- or five-credit course pattern were adopted, requirements could more appropriately be phrased in reference to courses rather than credits. The four-credit pattern is sometimes regarded as inefficient in use of classroom space, but by arranging sessions on alternate days, five four-credit courses can be accommodated in four classrooms. It is also possible to use periods of length greater than the usual fifty minutes and have only two or three class meetings.

education without forcing them into unreasonable competition with students better grounded in the area.

(16) Department credit offerings should not exceed forty semester credit hours (excluding the offerings suggested in 11 and 15).

(17) At least eighteen hours of the department major of thirty to forty hours should be a common requirement for all majors in the department.

(18) One or more courses in each department should be designated as independent study, thereby permitting emphasis or specialization appropriate for individuals or small groups of students. Many of the advanced courses now listed in departments could be dropped and considered as possible areas of independent study.

(19) The maximum number of credits from any single department acceptable for a degree should be forty.

(20) Every department major statement should include delineation of areas appropriate for supporting study, not so much in terms of specific courses as in terms of blocs of relevant knowledge, abilities, and skills.

(21) The objectives or levels of competency required for enrollment in and for credit in each course should be defined in sufficiently clear terms so that students may be properly placed and granted full credit for achievement, however attained.[2]

An institutional philosophy of education, the two-way chart, and the dimensions of Dressel's mathematical model provide parameters for the undergraduate curriculum. The creative part of curriculum-building then becomes the precision with which the important emerging elements to be included can be rationally identified.

The need for a theory of curriculum has been argued and some of the steps toward the development of a theory have been suggested. A theory of the curriculum transcends any particular curriculum or any particular educational philosophy. It deals with the nature of the curriculum in its generic sense, ways in which

[2] P. L. Dressel, *The Undergraduate Curriculum in Higher Education* (New York: Center for Applied Research in Education, 1963), pp. 83–85.

curricula come into being and perpetuate themselves, ways in which curricula change, and ways in which the appropriateness of curricula can be judged. Higher education today does not have the benefit of a fully developed theory to serve as a guide in curriculum matters, but hopefully this situation will be remedied before too long a time has passed.

Index

A new book in
THE JOSSEY-BASS SERIES
IN HIGHER EDUCATION

changing the curriculum

The contemporary college student needs and can have a contemporary curriculum. Despite research and experimentation in the past decade, the present curriculum remains essentially the same as it was in the 1930s. The climate is right for change. In *Changing the Curriculum*, Mayhew and Ford bring together a survey of the issues involved in change, an analysis of current curriculum practices, a study of today's student, specific suggestions for curriculum innovation, and a statement of the principles for solving curriculum problems. And from this background they develop the postulates for a broad curriculum theory—the basis for a dynamic new undergraduate curriculum.

Higher education today is a major paradox. It is conducted in a society experiencing perhaps the most revolutionary changes in the history of mankind. Yet the processes and practices of college education have not kept pace. It is obvious that changes—focusing on the undergraduate curriculum—are in order and can be accomplished. What these changes should be, how they can be thought about,

(continued on back flap)